T0049841

STAR WARS

CHARACTER
ENCYCLOPEDIA

UPDATED AND
EXPANDED EDITION

WRITTEN BY
**SIMON BEECROFT, ELIZABETH DOWSETT,
PABLO HIDALGO, AMY RICHAU, AND DAN ZEHR**

CONTENTS

Who stole the Death Star plans? Which droid became a ruthless bounty hunter? Who can breathe on land and underwater? The galaxy is full of heroes, villains, aliens, and droids. All have played a part—large or small—in the events of the dying days of the Galactic Republic, the battles of the Clone Wars, the desperate rebellion against the Empire, and the rise of the First Order.

FINDING A CHARACTER

Look up characters alphabetically by their first name or title, or use the index on page 286.

KEY TO ABBREVIATIONS IN DATA FILES

I: *Star Wars*: Episode I *The Phantom Menace*
II: *Star Wars*: Episode II *Attack of the Clones*
III: *Star Wars*: Episode III *Revenge of the Sith*
S: *Solo: A Star Wars Story*
RO: *Rogue One: A Star Wars Story*
IV: *Star Wars*: Episode IV *A New Hope*
V: *Star Wars*: Episode V *The Empire Strikes Back*
VI: *Star Wars*: Episode VI *Return of the Jedi*
M: *Star Wars: The Mandalorian*
VII: *Star Wars*: Episode VII *The Force Awakens*
VIII: *Star Wars*: Episode VIII *The Last Jedi*
IX: *Star Wars*: Episode IX *The Rise of Skywalker*

2-1B

SURGICAL DROID

DATA FILE

AFFILIATION: None
TYPE: Surgical droid
MANUFACTURER:
Industrial Automaton
HEIGHT: 1.77m (5ft 10in)
APPEARANCES: III, S, V, VI
SEE ALSO: Darth Vader; Luke Skywalker

Vocabulator

Transparent shell over hydraulics

Hydraulic leg

Stabilizing foot

SURGICAL DROIDS in the 2-1B

series are equipped with encyclopedic memory banks. They ensure that the droids give the best course of treatment in any medical situation.

2-1B MEDICAL and surgical droids have been around since Republic times. One such unit is attached to the rebel base on Hoth. He treats the injuries of many rebel troops, including Luke Skywalker after a wampa attacks him.

A Republic-era 2-1B droid rebuilds Darth Vader's burned body.

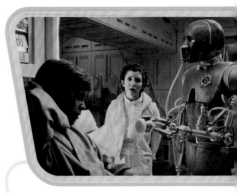

Rebel Surgeon

2-1B is able to perform extremely precise operations that leave little or no scar. The droid's long experience with humans makes him a caring medic. Luke Skywalker is so impressed with 2-1B's skills, he requests that the droid treats him again after he loses his hand on Cloud City.

4-LOM

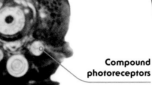

Compound photoreceptors

After the Battle of Hoth, Darth Vader hires 4-LOM and others to locate the *Millennium Falcon*.

DATA FILE

AFFILIATION: Bounty hunter
TYPE: LOM-series protocol droid
MANUFACTURER: Industrial Automaton
HEIGHT: 1.67m (5ft 6in)
APPEARANCES: V
SEE ALSO: Darth Vader; Jabba the Hutt; Zuckuss

BlasTech DLT-19 heavy blaster rifle

Battered black droid plating

THIS HUMANOID DROID with an insectlike face used to be a sophisticated protocol droid made to resemble the species he served. 4-LOM was once assigned to a luxury liner, but his programming was overwritten and he began a life of crime as a bounty hunter.

THE PERSONALITY

software corruption that transformed 4-LOM into a deadly bounty hunter is a known flaw in the LOM-series. Other similarly affected protocol droids of the same make have been spotted working as enforcers in the Outer Rim Territories.

Dangerous Duo

4-LOM often works in partnership with a bounty hunter named Zuckuss. The combination of 4-LOM's powers of deduction and analysis with Zuckuss' mystical intuition makes their collaboration successful and lucrative.

AAYLA SECURA

TWI'LEK JEDI KNIGHT

DATA FILE

AFFILIATION: Jedi
HOMEWORLD: Ryloth
SPECIES: Twi'lek
HEIGHT: 1.7m (5ft 7in)
APPEARANCES: II, III
SEE ALSO: Ahsoka Tano;
Kit Fisto; Mace Windu; Yoda

Lightsaber powered by a blue kyber crystal

Lekku (head-tail)

CUNNING AAYLA SECURA is a Twi'lek Jedi Knight who relies on her athletic lightsaber skills to outwit opponents. As a Jedi general, Aayla leads a squad of clone troopers on many campaigns.

Belt made of rycrit hide

AAYLA SECURA is an intelligent, sometimes mischievous Jedi. Her teacher was a troubled Jedi named Quinlan Vos. Aayla passes on the teachings of her master to young Ahsoka Tano during a Clone Wars mission that goes awry, and ends up on the grassland planet of Maridun.

Fitted clothing allows complete freedom of movement

Secura's own clone troopers turn on her on Felucia.

Captured

At the Battle of Geonosis, Aayla Secura is among the circle of Jedi captured by Geonosian soldiers. Luckily, clone trooper reinforcements come to their rescue.

ADI GALLIA

THOLOTHIAN JEDI MASTER

DATA FILE

AFFILIATION: Jedi
HOMEWORLD: Coruscant
SPECIES: Tholothian
HEIGHT: 1.84m (6ft)
APPEARANCES: I, II
SEE ALSO: Bail Organa;
Chancellor Valorum; Eeth
Koth; Even Piell; Stass Allie

JEDI MASTER ADI GALLIA was born into a high-ranking diplomatic family stationed on Coruscant. Gallia is a Jedi High Council member and a noble general in the Clone Wars.

Long, fleshy tendrils descend from scaled cranium

Jedi robe

Lightsaber

Utility pouch

As a High Council member, Adi Gallia is respected for her powers of intuition.

Tall travel boots

ADI GALLIA is a valuable intelligence source to Senate leaders. Her life is cut short in the Clone Wars when she is killed by the renegade Nightbrother Savage Opress.

Jedi Temple
Gallia may be stationed at the Jedi Temple on Coruscant, but the events of the Clone Wars send her to battlefronts across the galaxy. She helps rescue Master Eeth Koth after his capture by General Grievous over Saleucami.

ADMIRAL ACKBAR

RESISTANCE SPACE FORCE ADMIRAL

DATA FILE

AFFILIATION: Rebel Alliance; Resistance
HOMEWORLD: Mon Cala
SPECIES: Mon Calamari
HEIGHT: 1.8m (5ft 11in)
APPEARANCES: VI, VII, VIII
SEE ALSO: Aftab Ackbar; General Madine; Mon Mothma; Princess Leia

ADMIRAL GIAL Ackbar was born on the ocean world of Mon Cala. A veteran of the Clone Wars, he is later instrumental in bringing his people into the Rebel Alliance. After the Galactic Civil War, he is coaxed out of retirement by Princess Leia to join the Resistance during the rise of the First Order.

Rank badge

Waterproof skin

Belt clasp

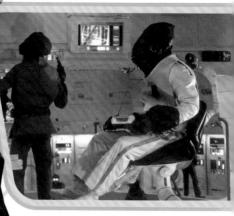

Ackbar commands the rebel fleet from his personal flagship, *Home One*.

AS COMMANDER of the rebel fleet, Admiral Ackbar plans and leads the attack on the Empire's capital ships at the Battle of Endor.

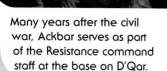

Many years after the civil war, Ackbar serves as part of the Resistance command staff at the base on D'Qar.

Home One

Ackbar's people contribute their giant Mon Cal star cruisers to the Alliance. *Home One* serves as a mobile command center after the Empire discovers and destroys the main Alliance headquarters on Hoth.

ADMIRAL OZZEL

ADMIRAL OF THE *EXECUTOR*

DATA FILE

AFFILIATION: Empire
HOMEWORLD: Carida
SPECIES: Human
HEIGHT: 1.75m (5ft 9in)
APPEARANCES: V
SEE ALSO: Admiral Piett;
Darth Vader; General Veers

Officer's disk

KENDAL OZZEL is the commander of Darth Vader's gigantic flagship, the *Executor*. Under Ozzel's sometimes uncertain command, the *Executor* emerges from hyperspace too close to Hoth, alerting the rebels to the Imperials' presence.

Imperial code cylinder

Rank insignia plaque

KENDAL OZZEL

serves in the Republic Navy during the Clone Wars and soon works his way up the military ladder. Ozzel is ambitious but displays poor judgment and ineffective tactical thinking, which he attempts to mask with his authoritarian persona.

Belt buckle contains secret data-storage compartment

The *Executor* leads Darth Vader's personal fleet of Star Destroyers, known as the Death Squadron.

Deadly Blunders

Vader's view of Ozzel is that he is "as clumsy as he is stupid." After a series of blunders by Ozzel—first, doubting evidence of life on Hoth, then the failed attempt to surprise the rebels—Vader Force-chokes Ozzel and promotes Captain Piett to admiral in Ozzel's place.

Durasteel-toed boots

ADMIRAL PIETT

COMMANDER OF THE *EXECUTOR*

DATA FILE

AFFILIATION: Empire
HOMEWORLD: Axxila
SPECIES: Human
HEIGHT: 1.73m (5ft 8in)
APPEARANCES: V, VI
SEE ALSO: Admiral Ozzel;
Darth Vader

An A-wing destroys the *Executor's* bridge, killing the crew and crashing the ship.

Naval officer's tunic

PIETT IS A loyal Imperial captain on Darth Vader's flagship, the *Executor*. After Vader Force-chokes Admiral Ozzel to death for incompetence, Piett is instantly promoted to admiral of the fleet. Piett loses his life when a rebel A-wing crashes through the bridge of the *Executor*.

Leather gloves

UNLIKE MOST Imperial officers, who come from the prestigious Inner Core worlds, Firmus Piett has his origins in the Outer Rim. He is known for his quick thinking and his ability to shift blame for mistakes he has made.

Risky Strategy

Vader's officers must submit entirely to the Dark Lord's iron will. When Vader insists that Piett makes a risky pursuit of the *Millennium Falcon* into an asteroid field, Piett nervously does Vader's bidding, aware that errors could lead to his death.

ADMIRAL RADDUS

MON CALAMARI COMMANDER OF THE FLEET

DATA FILE

AFFILIATION: Rebel Alliance
HOMEWORLD: Mon Cala
SPECIES: Mon Calamari
HEIGHT: 1.9m (6ft 3in)
APPEARANCES: RO
SEE ALSO: Admiral
Ackbar; General Merrick;
Princess Leia

Fishlike eyes see well on
land and under water

ADMIRAL RADDUS was an
early recruit to the rebel cause
when the Empire overran
his aquatic homeworld,
Mon Cala. Stern and
steely, Raddus
makes a determined
and dedicated
fleet commander.

Waterproof datapad
with orders

Mon Cala civic
crest awarded for
planetary defense

RADDUS HAS

experience of city defense and
leadership skills he honed as
Mayor of Nystullum. He also
gives the fledgling Alliance
fleet the *Profundity*, a city-ship,
now converted into a warship.

Raddus is not one to shy from
battle. When he hears of the
rogue Scarif mission, he leaps
to their support.

Honored Hero

Raddus' direct and pragmatic manner
does not endear him to everyone.
But such is his contribution and sacrifice
to the Rebellion, many years later,
General Leia Organa's star cruiser is
named the *Raddus*, in his honor.

ADMIRAL STATURA

RESISTANCE OFFICER

DATA FILE

AFFILIATION: Resistance
HOMEWORLD: Garel
SPECIES: Human
HEIGHT: 1.72m (5ft 8in)
APPEARANCES: VII
SEE ALSO: Admiral
Ackbar; General Ematt;
Princess Leia

USHOS O. STATURA was only a teenager when the war against the Galactic Empire ended, but he experienced combat firsthand while trying to liberate his homeworld from Imperial rule. He loyally serves General Leia Organa.

Repurposed Rebel
Alliance crest

Admiral's rank badge

WHEN GENERAL Organa assembled trusted military advisors to form the core of her Resistance movement, she turned to experienced rebel veterans. Statura was younger than most, and plucked from a career in applied sciences.

Statura watches the battle above the Starkiller unfold from the Resistance command center on D'Qar.

Battle Analysis

Statura is practical and technically minded, traits he uses well in his role supervising logistics for the Resistance. He keenly assesses the Starkiller threat, correctly guessing the unimaginable scale of its destructive power. It is his analysis that leads to the Resistance starfighter attack on the weapon.

AFTAB ACKBAR

RESISTANCE Y-WING PILOT

DATA FILE

AFFILIATION: Resistance
HOMEWORLD: Mon Cala
SPECIES: Mon Calamari
HEIGHT: 1.8m (5ft 11in)
APPEARANCES: IX
SEE ALSO: Admiral Ackbar;
Beaumont Kin; Kaydel
Connix; Larma D'Acy;
Rose Tico; Snap Wexley

Eyes have
180-degree vision

AFTAB ACKBAR joins the
Resistance to honor his father,
Admiral Gial Ackbar, who died
fighting the First Order. He is
a colonel in the Resistance
and flies a Y-wing when
the Resistance fleet
departs Ajan Kloss.

Life-support unit

Flight harness

AFTAB MET his father only
once, but he has studied every one of
his battles and victories. Aftab helps
Leia Organa and Rey when they
travel to Mon Cala to rekindle
Leia's old alliance with his people.

Aftab follows General Poe
Dameron's orders during
the Battle of Exegol.

New Connections

Aftab is quick to befriend other
members of the Resistance, including
historian Beaumont Kin and X-wing
pilot Snap Wexley. He mourns with his
new Resistance family after the death
of General Leia Organa.

Boots customized
to fit webbed feet

AGEN KOLAR

ZABRAK JEDI MASTER

DATA FILE

AFFILIATION: Jedi
HOMEWORLD: Iridonia
SPECIES: Zabrak
HEIGHT: 1.9m (6ft 3in)
APPEARANCES: II, III
SEE ALSO: Kit Fisto;
Mace Windu; Saesee Tiin

Horns regenerate over time

Lightsaber uses dual crystals to create green or blue energy blades

Two-handed ready stance

AGEN KOLAR is a master swordsmith who joins the Jedi Knights that battle the Separatist Army on Geonosis. Mace Windu has a high opinion of Kolar's combat skills and enlists him in a desperate attempt to arrest Supreme Chancellor Palpatine.

AGEN KOLAR is a Zabrak, as is fellow Jedi Eeth Koth. The Zabrak species is identified by its head horns. Known to strike first and ask questions later, Kolar is also a valuable member of the Jedi High Council.

Hooded robe often removed in combat

Agen Kolar's renowned lightsaber skills are put to use on Geonosis.

Skillful Sith

Even the celebrated sword skills of Agen Kolar cannot match the speed and unsparing power of a Sith Lord such as Darth Sidious.

14

AHSOKA TANO

LIGHT SIDE WARRIOR

DATA FILE

AFFILIATION: Jedi (former); Rebel Alliance

HOMEWORLD: Unknown

SPECIES: Togruta

HEIGHT: 1.76m (5ft 9in)

APPEARANCES: M

SEE ALSO: Anakin Skywalker; Bo-Katan Kryze; Grogu

FORMER PADAWAN of Anakin Skywalker, Ahsoka Tano leaves the Jedi Order but never abandons the light side of the Force. Ahsoka is a fierce combatant but an even better friend, and is as kind as she is courageous when helping those in need.

Lightsaber powered by a purified white kyber crystal

Intricate pattern on belt buckle

AFTER ORDER 66,

Ahsoka Tano goes into hiding until she is enlisted by Bail Organa to help find others who will stand up to the tyranny of the Empire. She takes on the nickname "Fulcrum" and recruits many heroes to the Rebellion.

Showdown

Ahsoka faces a grueling duel on the planet Corvus with Magistrate Morgan Elsbeth. She demands that Elsbeth reveal the location of her master, Grand Admiral Thrawn. Elsbeth is a worthy opponent but is no match for Ahsoka's Jedi training.

Ahsoka and Grogu form a bond as he shares his story with her.

ALAZMEC COLONIST

PROTECTORS OF VADER'S CASTLE

Orange-tinted
night-vision lenses

THE ALAZMEC OF WINSIT are
Sith cultists who have settled
on the volcanic planet
Mustafar. They honor Darth
Vader and protect the
ruins of his castle and a
nearby bog named
Corvax Fen. The Alazmec
refuse passage through
the bog to everyone,
including Kylo Ren.

Weather-resistant poncho

CX-55
scatterblaster

AFTER CENTURIES of
volcanic activity, some parts of
Mustafar are beginning to cool and
show signs of life. The Alazmec plant
irontrees around the Corvax Fen and
care for them as they search for a
connection to the power of the Sith.

Chilling attack

Supreme Leader Kylo Ren travels to
Mustafar to search for clues to Emperor
Palpatine's whereabouts. After slaying
the Alazmec colonists, Ren discovers an
ancient artifact called a Sith wayfinder
in the ruins of Darth Vader's castle.
The wayfinder leads Ren to Palpatine's
location, the planet Exegol.

Canvas leg
covering

The crude weapons of the
Alazmec are no match for
the lightsaber skills of
Supreme Leader Kylo Ren.

ALBREKH

DATA FILE

AFFILIATION: First Order; Sith
HOMEWORLD: Unknown
SPECIES: Symeong
HEIGHT: 1.52m (5ft)
APPEARANCES: IX
SEE ALSO: Ap'lek;
Cardo; Kuruk; Kylo Ren;
Trudgen; Ushar; Vicrul

ALBREKH IS A gruff Sith alchemist enlisted by the First Order to repair Supreme Leader Kylo Ren's helmet. He carefully forges the helmet pieces together with a red ore, and the reforged helmet is stronger than it was before.

Goggles help with finer work

Alchemical instruments

ALBREKH'S SKILL in alchemy
makes it possible for him to fix items others believe to be beyond repair. His steady hands and precise movements are not affected by the watchful eyes of the fearsome Knights of Ren.

Albrekh uses an ancient device called a Sith forge in his work for Kylo Ren.

Careful Craftsmanship
The alchemist uses red Sarrassian iron, found in the Aniras asteroid belt, to reforge Kylo Ren's helmet. Ancient Sith alchemists believed Sarrassian iron to contain special particles that call to the dark side of the Force.

Oilcloth boots

ALLEGIANT GENERAL PRYDE

ARROGANT FIRST ORDER COMMANDER

DATA FILE

AFFILIATION: Empire; First Order
HOMEWORLD: Alsakan
SPECIES: Human
HEIGHT: 1.88m (6ft 2in)
APPEARANCES: IX
SEE ALSO: General Hux; Kylo Ren; Palpatine

INTELLIGENT AND RUTHLESS, Enric Pryde commands a fleet of deadly Star Destroyers in the First Order navy. He yearns for the return of a galaxy-wide dictatorship like the Galactic Empire he once served.

First Order patch

Belt from Pryde's last Imperial uniform

PRYDE DOES not understand the Force, but knows its power, having seen Darth Vader in action. Kylo Ren and Palpatine reward Pryde's loyalty to the dark side by promoting him to the rank of allegiant general—which gives him control of both ground and space forces.

Perfectly pressed tunic

Power Hungry

Pryde detests General Hux, despite his previous good relationship with Hux's father. Pryde relishes being a superior to Hux on the flagship Star Destroyer *Steadfast*. He is quick to execute his rival when he discovers Hux has betrayed Kylo Ren and the First Order.

Palpatine instructs Pryde to deploy the Sith fleet, called the Final Order.

ANAKIN SKYWALKER

LEGENDARY JEDI KNIGHT

DATA FILE

AFFILIATION: Jedi; Republic
HOMEWORLD: Tatooine
SPECIES: Human
HEIGHT: 1.85m (6ft 1in)
APPEARANCES: I, II, III, VI
SEE ALSO: Obi-Wan Kenobi; Padmé Amidala; Qui-Gon Jinn

Gauntlet covers mechno-hand (which replaces hand sliced off by Count Dooku)

Jedi utility belt

Young Anakin's keen perception and unnaturally fast reflexes show his great Force potential.

ANAKIN SKYWALKER'S rise to power is astonishing. In a few short years, he goes from being enslaved on Tatooine to becoming one of the most powerful Jedi ever. But Anakin's thirst for power leads him to the dark side of the Force, with tragic consequences for the galaxy.

IN THE CLONE WARS, Anakin loses his faith in the Jedi to restore peace and harmony to the galaxy. He also feels great anger at the tragic death of his mother and fears that the same fate may befall Padmé Amidala (who is secretly his wife). Finally, Anakin is persuaded that only the dark side can give him the power to prevent death.

Close Bond

Anakin's bond with his teacher, Obi-Wan Kenobi, is strong. They make a dynamic team in the Clone Wars, where Anakin proves to be a great leader. Yet Anakin is troubled by feelings of anger and mistrust.

Anakin's impulsive nature leads him toward the dark side.

AP'LEK

KNIGHT OF REN STRATEGIST

All Knights of Ren wear black

Oiled cloth is waterproof

Beskar steel blade

Lying in Wait

Ap'lek prepares to capture Chewbacca to transport him back to the First Order. Ap'lek's weapon of choice is an ancient Mandalorian executioner's ax.

AP'LEK IS THE most strategic of the six Knights of Ren, who all serve Kylo Ren. Ap'lek enjoys deceiving his targets (and occasionally his fellow Knights) on missions.

AP'LEK'S BELT includes a smoke dispenser. Like all the Knights of Ren, Ap'lek is Force sensitive, which allows him to sense his prey through the smoke.

Customized shin armor

Ap'lek believes his cunning and intelligence to be far superior to his fellow Knights of Ren.

20

THE ARMORER

DATA FILE

AFFILIATION: Nevarro Mandalorian covert
HOMEWORLD: Mandalore
SPECIES: Unknown
HEIGHT: 1.7m (5ft 7in)
APPEARANCES: M
SEE ALSO: Grogu; the Mandalorian; Paz Vizsla

Beskar helmet

The Armorer informs Din Djarin that the beskar he retrieved will help many aspiring Mandalorians.

Cuirass with bronzium finish

Protective gloves

THE ARMORER on Nevarro crafts weapons and armor for Children of the Watch, an ancient Mandalorian belief system for followers of the Way. Wise and powerful, she helps guide Din Djarin.

Blacksmith

Among her many talents, the Armorer molds and shapes beskar, a rare Mandalorian metal, into armor and weapons for the members of the covert she leads. These skills help protect the group physically, but her mentorship and wisdom are equally treasured.

IN THE sewers underneath Nevarro City, the Armorer provides the Mandalorians with guidance and refills ammunitions. She calmly helps each member search for their signet, a symbol that helps define each Mandalorian's true calling.

Fireproof boots

21

ARTILLERY STORMTROOPER

HEAVY WEAPONS EXPERTS

DATA FILE

AFFILIATION: Empire; Imperial Remnant
HOMEWORLD: Varies
SPECIES: Human
HEIGHT (AVG.): 1.83m (6ft)
STANDARD EQUIPMENT: Model 201 mortar
APPEARANCES: M
SEE ALSO: Moff Gideon

Yellow markings indicate artillery trooper specialist

Thermal detonator

WHEN THE EMPIRE needs extra firepower, they send in artillery stormtroopers. These specialized soldiers launch explosives high into the air with pinpoint accuracy.

ALSO KNOWN as shell troopers, artillery stormtroopers are highly skilled with explosives. They are able to keep cool and think quickly in intense combat.

The Big Guns

On Tython, Moff Gideon sends stormtroopers to capture Grogu and eliminate the Mandalorian. An artillery stormtrooper launches an explosive at the bounty hunter and his companions during the attack.

Collapsible Merr-Sonn Munitions Model 201 mortar

Specially designed backpacks contain canister-shaped thermal detonators.

AT-AT PILOT

DATA FILE

AFFILIATION: Empire
HOMEWORLD: Varies
SPECIES: Human
HEIGHT (AVG.): 1.83m (6ft)
STANDARD EQUIPMENT:
Blaster pistol; thermal
detonators; grenades
APPEARANCES: V
SEE ALSO: AT-ST pilot;
General Veers

ONLY A SMALL number of
Imperial combat drivers are put
forward for training to become
pilots of the terrifying All Terrain
Armored Transport (AT-AT)
walkers. AT-AT pilots, who
generally work in pairs,
consider themselves
all-powerful.

Reinforced helmet

Life-support pack

Insulated jumpsuit

AT-ATs are not climate
controlled, so pilots wear special
insulated suits on frozen planets
such as Hoth. The suits protect
the wearer if the walker's
pressurized cockpit is smashed
open in hostile environments.

Driving gauntlet

The pilots sit in the cockpit in
the AT-AT's head, operating
driving and firing controls.

Walking Terror
The giant AT-AT walkers march
relentlessly across uneven
battlegrounds, using their mighty
laser cannons to wreak destruction
on the enemy forces below.

AT-ST PILOT

DATA FILE

AFFILIATION: Empire
HOMEWORLD: Varies
SPECIES: Human
HEIGHT (AVG.): 1.83m (6ft)
STANDARD EQUIPMENT:
Blasters; thermal detonators
APPEARANCES: V, VI
SEE ALSO: AT-AT pilot;
Chewbacca

AT-STs are equipped with two powerful medium blaster cannons.

Jumpsuit

TWO-LEGGED AT-ST

(All Terrain Scout Transport) walkers march into battle, spraying blaster bolts at enemy troops. Each walker houses two highly trained pilots with superior skills of balance and agility.

Fire-resistant gauntlet

AT-ST PILOTS wear

open-face helmets, blast goggles, and basic armor plating under their jumpsuits. During the Battle of Endor, AT-ST walkers are deployed against the rebels. Many are lost to surprise attacks by Ewoks.

Two pilots keep the AT-ST walker moving at speed through uneven terrain.

On the Hunt

AT-ST walkers are used on reconnaissance and anti-personnel hunting missions. They are not invulnerable to attack, as Chewbacca demonstrates when he forces his way inside a walker through the roof.

AURRA SING

VICIOUS BOUNTY HUNTER

DATA FILE

AFFILIATION: Bounty hunter
HOMEWORLD: Nar Shaddaa
SPECIES: Palliduvan
HEIGHT: 1.83m (6ft)
APPEARANCES: I
SEE ALSO: Boba Fett; Bossk; Padmé Amidala

AURRA SING is a ruthless bounty hunter. A seemingly ageless veteran of the underworld scene, she worked with such contemporaries as Jango Fett and Cad Bane. During the Clone Wars, she was hired by Ziro the Hutt to assassinate Padmé Amidala. She is rumored to have fallen in a duel with smuggler Tobias Beckett.

AURRA SING was born in the polluted urban sprawl of Nar Shaddaa. She never knew her father, and her mother was too poor to raise her. Sing became a cold-blooded killer. She is willing to use any means necessary to locate her prey. She has sensor implants and has a wide assortment of weapons in her private arsenal, including lightsabers and a sniper's projectile rifle.

Short-range pistol

Long fingers to draw blood

Long-range projectile rifle

During the Clone Wars, Aurra guides the recently orphaned Boba Fett.

High Alert

On the trail of her quarry on Tatooine, Aurra Sing is a spectator at the podrace that will earn young Anakin Skywalker his freedom.

AXE WOVES

MANDALORIAN LOYALIST

DATA FILE

AFFILIATION: Mandalorians
HOMEWORLD: Mandalore
SPECIES: Human
HEIGHT: 1.8m (5ft 11in)
APPEARANCES: M
SEE ALSO: Bo-Katan
Kryze; Koska Reeves

AXE WOVES WORKS with Bo-Katan Kryze and Koska Reeves to regain control of their homeworld, Mandalore, and help Bo-Katan find the Darksaber. Woves is dedicated to his planet and people.

Mandalorian breastplate

Vambrace with compartment for data spike

Silver buckle with hidden compartment

Hidden blaster under gauntlet

AXE WEARS blue-and-gray Mandalorian armor and is a powerful warrior. He is skilled in hand-to-hand combat and with multiple types of weapons. Although Woves jokes that stormtroopers are poor shots, he does not take his enemies lightly.

Axe Woves uses a data spike to open a door into the Imperial ship.

Team Up

Axe wants to return Mandalore to the way it was before the Empire. His team works with Din Djarin to capture an Imperial freighter and plans a way to defeat their mutual enemy.

BABU FRIK

BLACK MARKET DROIDSMITH

DATA FILE

AFFILIATION: Spice Runners of Kijimi
HOMEWORLD: Kijimi
SPECIES: Anzellan
HEIGHT: 22cm (9in)
APPEARANCES: IX
SEE ALSO: C-3PO; Poe Dameron; Zorii Bliss

Welding mask

Eyes can see microscopic details

Protective leather hood

Heating torch

THE TALENTED DROIDSMITH Babu Frik can reprogram or modify most droids. A member of the Spice Runners of Kijimi crew led by Zorii Bliss, Babu's small size helps him avoid detection by First Order troops.

Babu Frik and Zorii Bliss join Poe Dameron and the Resistance fleet to take on the Sith Eternal's forces.

BABU FRIK takes great pride in his work, regardless of whether the job is legal or not. The droidsmith has a working knowledge of Basic, but prefers to communicate with as few words as possible unless speaking Anzellan to his boss, Zorii Bliss.

Mind Wipe

Babu Frik has to erase C-3PO's memories in order to bypass restrictions preventing the droid from translating Sith inscriptions for Rey. Babu always tries to befriend the droids he's working on to keep them at ease.

BAIL ORGANA

VICEROY OF ALDERAAN

DATA FILE

AFFILIATION: Republic; Rebel Alliance
HOMEWORLD: Alderaan
SPECIES: Human
HEIGHT: 1.91m (6ft 3in)
APPEARANCES: II, III, RO
SEE ALSO: Mon Mothma; Princess Leia

Alderaanian cloak

Target blaster

Action boots

Bail and his wife, Breha, adopt Leia after Padmé's death.

BAIL ORGANA is the Senator for Alderaan. He watches, horrified, as the Galactic Republic becomes a dictatorship under Palpatine. Along with Mon Mothma, Bail is one of the founders of the Rebellion against Emperor Palpatine.

Alderaanian belt

ORGANA remains loyal to the Republic and the Jedi Order to the end. In Imperial times, it is Bail who responds to the threat of the Death Star by sending his adopted daughter, Leia, on a mission to locate Obi-Wan Kenobi in order to recruit him to the Rebel Alliance.

After Order 66, Bail assists any survivors that he can.

Influential Contact

When the rebels learn of the Death Star threat, Mon Mothma turns to Bail for help. An old friend of his is a Jedi in hiding, and Bail's daughter, Princess Leia, might be able to track him down.

BALA-TIK

GUAVIAN FRONTMAN

DATA FILE

AFFILIATION: Guavian Death Gang
HOMEWORLD: Unknown
SPECIES: Human
HEIGHT: 1.8m (5ft 11in)
APPEARANCES: VII
SEE ALSO: Guavian Security Soldier; Han Solo; Kanjiklub gang; Tasu Leech

AN AGENT FOR the Guavian Death Gang, Bala-Tik's patience with Han Solo has been worn out by one too many excuses for failed payments. Bala-Tik brings a group of security soldiers with him to collect what is due from Han.

Armored lining in coat

Gorraslug-leather coat

Percussive cannon

Bala-Tik and the rest of the Guavians carry black market technology, such as experimental percussive cannons.

THE GUAVIAN enforcers are faceless, voiceless cybernetic soldiers, so they rely on Bala-Tik to act as the negotiator in tense confrontations. In the past, Bala-Tik has often been willing to let Solo go, since the Corellian is a good source of money-making leads.

Hunting Solo

Bala-Tik's bosses have ordered him to make an example of Solo. He forges an unlikely alliance with the Kanjiklub gang as they are also owed tens of thousands of credits by Han. After hunting down Solo, Bala-Tik discovers a droid in Solo's possession that the First Order is searching for, and sees an irresistible opportunity to profit.

BARRISS OFFEE

MIRIALAN PADAWAN AND TRAITOR

DATA FILE

AFFILIATION: Jedi
HOMEWORLD: Mirial
SPECIES: Mirialan
HEIGHT: 1.66m (5ft 5in)
APPEARANCES: II
SEE ALSO: Ahsoka Tano;
Luminara Unduli; Shaak Ti

PADAWAN BARRISS OFFEE is a thoughtful, daring, and studious Jedi. She is the Padawan learner of Master Luminara Unduli. Barriss is a loyal apprentice who adheres closely to the Jedi Code until the trials of the Clone Wars change her point of view.

Mirialan tattoos

Two-handed grip for control

BARRISS OFFEE came to view the Jedi role in the Clone Wars as a betrayal of the Order's ideals. She lashes out against her own kind in a violent manner, orchestrating a bombing of the Jedi Temple and framing fellow Padawan Ahsoka Tano for the crime. Barriss is discovered and imprisoned.

Belt contains secret compartment

Offee was one of the many Jedi present at the Battle of Geonosis.

Hooded robe

Powerful Team

Offee specialized in tandem fighting and used the Force to keep her actions perfectly in sync with her partner Unduli. The team of Unduli and Offee was more powerful than the sum of its parts.

BATTLE DROID

MECHANICAL DROID SOLDIERS

Simple vocoder

Arm extension piston

Battle droids are first deployed against the peaceful people of Naboo.

E-5 blaster rifle

BATTLE DROIDS are the ground troops of the Separatist army and are designed to resemble their Geonosian creators. The later B1 droids are capable of independent thought and can exhibit emotions.

BATTLE DROIDS are intended to win by strength of numbers rather than by individual ability. Early models of these mass-produced droids are unable to think independently, so a computer on board a Trade Federation ship feeds them all their mission commands.

Folding knee joint

Limbs resemble humanoid skeletons

Pilot droids operate the vast Separatist fleets.

STAPs

Battle droid scouts and snipers are swept through the air on armed Single Trooper Aerial Platforms, or STAPs. These repulsorlift vehicles can thread through dense forests that would be inaccessible to larger vehicles.

BAZE MALBUS

REBEL EXTREMIST

Cooling tank

DATA FILE

AFFILIATION Guardian of the Whills (former)
HOMEWORLD: Jedha
SPECIES: Human
HEIGHT: 1.8m (5ft 11in)
APPEARANCES: RO
SEE ALSO: Bodhi Rook; Cassian Andor; Chirrut Îmwe; Jyn Erso; K-2SO

A BATTLE-HARDENED warrior, Baze operates in Jedha's murky underworld. He takes no interest in politics until the Empire affects him personally. Driven by a thirst for retribution, he joins the Rogue One mission.

Plastoid polymer armor

MWC-35c Staccato Lightning repeating cannon

Weatherproof cloak

Baze and Chirrut Îmwe have conflicting outlooks, but get along well together.

Armored pad for kneeling

BAZE WAS once a Guardian of the Whills, but he abandoned his spiritual side long ago. Now he puts his faith in firepower, embracing modern heavy weapons. He would choose a rocket launcher over a traditional lightbow any day.

Firepower

Baze blasts his way across Scarif with his illegally modified repeating cannon. He puts himself in the firing line to distract the Imperial stormtroopers and shoretroopers while Jyn Erso and Cassian Andor retrieve the Death Star files from the Citadel Tower.

BAZINE NETAL

DEEP COVER SPY

DATA FILE

AFFILIATION: Independent
HOMEWORLD: Chaaktil
SPECIES: Human
HEIGHT: 1.7m (5ft 7in)
APPEARANCES: VII
SEE ALSO: Grummgar;
Kanjiklub gang; Maz Kanata

AN ALLURING and dangerous woman of intrigue lurking in the shadows of Maz Kanata's castle, Bazine Netal is a master of cloak and dagger. She uses her skills of deception to coax secrets from the unwitting and the unwilling.

Custom-styled light-absorbing shroud

Baffleweave patterning

Bazine sits with Grummgar, a big game hunter who frequents Maz Kanata's castle. From this vantage point, Bazine can see all that transpires in the castle.

BAZINE LEARNED

the fundamentals of self-defense living in the dangerous streets of Chaako City, the biggest urban center on Chaaktil. Bazine trained under Delphi Kloda, a grizzled former pirate Kanjiklubber who was the closest thing to a father she ever knew. As a result, Bazine is an expert in unarmed combat.

Vanishing Act

Though Bazine prefers to rely on her own skills rather than technology, she nonetheless keeps sophisticated tools in her arsenal. The complex patterns on her dress are lined with sensor-jamming baffleweave, an electronically impregnated fabric that causes her to disappear from scanner readings.

BB-8

POE DAMERON'S ASTROMECH DROID

DATA FILE

AFFILIATION: Resistance
TYPE: Astromech droid
MANUFACTURER: Industrial Automaton
HEIGHT: 67cm (2ft 2in)
APPEARANCES: VII, VIII, IX
SEE ALSO: Finn; Poe Dameron; R2-D2; Rey

High-frequency receiver antenna

Primary photoreceptor

Swappable tool bay

AN INTENSELY LOYAL astromech, BB-8 bravely rolls into danger, often on daring missions with Poe Dameron. He is the subject of an intense First Order search when he carries a part of a map that could lead to Luke Skywalker.

AS AN ASTROMECH droid, BB-8's small, spherical body is designed to fit into the droid socket of an X-wing starfighter. From that position BB-8 can manage the essential systems of the vessel, make repairs, and plot courses through space.

BB-8 speaks in beeps and whirs, and can project holograms.

Ball Droid

A complex drive system and wireless telemetry keep BB-8 on the move, tumbling his body forward while keeping his head upright. When situations require greater stability, BB-8 can deploy cables from compressed launchers that then anchor the droid in place, or allow him to reel himself into hard-to-reach places.

BEAUMONT KIN

RESISTANCE INTELLIGENCE CAPTAIN

BEAUMONT KIN IS an intelligence officer with the Resistance, but studying Jedi and Sith history is his passion. He uses his language skills and knowledge of the occult to aid Rey and other members of the Resistance in their battle against the First Order.

Insect-repelling fabric

Rank badge

AFTER THE destruction of the Hosnian system, Kin puts his plans to become a professor on hold and joins the Resistance. He's quick to suspect that Emperor Palpatine's return is due to cloning or other forms of dark science.

Glie-44 blaster pistol

Kin, Rose Tico, and Kaydel Connix fight Sith troopers on the hull of the First Order Star Destroyer *Steadfast*.

Translation Expert

Kin is fluent in nine languages, including four ancient dialects. He speaks Shyriiwook while helping Chewbacca free Wookiees on Kashyyyk and later helps Rey translate ancient Jedi texts and notes from Luke Skywalker that she recovered from Ahch-To.

Pockets often hold important notes

BEN SOLO

DYAD IN THE FORCE WITH REY

DATA FILE

AFFILIATION: Jedi; Force
Dyad
HOMEWORLD: Chandrila
SPECIES: Human
HEIGHT: 1.89m (6ft 2in)
APPEARANCES: VII, VIII, IX
SEE ALSO: Han Solo; Princess
Leia; Palpatine; Supreme
Leader Snoke; Rey

Unkempt hair

THE SON OF HAN SOLO and
Leia Organa, Ben Solo spends
much of his life torn between
the light and dark sides of the
Force. After years embracing
the dark side as Kylo Ren, Ben
returns to the light to aid
Rey on Exegol.

Tattered outfit

PALPATINE uses Snoke,
his evil creation, to help turn
young Ben Solo to the dark
side. His uncle and Jedi Master,
Luke Skywalker, is unaware
Snoke is secretly speaking to
Ben until it is too late.

Force Dyad

Ben and Rey are a rare Dyad in the
Force—this unique and powerful Force
bond makes them stronger together
than apart. Ben saves Rey by giving
her his last life energy, even though
it means the end of his own life.

Ben wakes to find his uncle
seemingly ready to attack,
sensing the darkness in him.

Skywalker lightsaber

BERU LARS

DATA FILE

AFFILIATION: None
HOMEWORLD: Tatooine
SPECIES: Human
HEIGHT: 1.65m (5ft 5in)
APPEARANCES: II, III, IV
SEE ALSO: Luke Skywalker;
Owen Lars

Simple
hairstyle

BERU LARS' family has been
made up of moisture farmers
for three generations. At the
end of the Clone Wars,
Obi-Wan Kenobi asks Beru and
her husband, Owen, to
raise Luke Skywalker,
while he lives nearby
to watch over the boy.

Desert tunic

Beru meets Anakin Skywalker
when he investigates his
mother's kidnapping.

Rough clothing
made in Anchorhead

BERU LARS is hard-
working and self-reliant. She is
well equipped to deal with most
of the dangers encountered in
the Tatooine desert. However,
nothing can prepare Beru for the
group of Imperial stormtroopers
who come in search of the two
renegade droids carrying the
stolen Death Star plans.

Protector

As Luke becomes a young adult, Beru
understands his desire to leave home
and join the Imperial academy. But
she also knows the truth about Luke's
father, and respects Owen's desire
to protect Luke from following in
Anakin's footsteps.

Desert boots

BIB FORTUNA

CRIMINAL OVERLORD

DATA FILE

AFFILIATION: Criminal underworld
HOMEWORLD: Ryloth
SPECIES: Twi'lek
HEIGHT: 2m (6ft 7in)
APPEARANCES: I, VI, M
SEE ALSO: Jabba the Hutt

THE SINISTER BIB FORTUNA oversees the day-to-day affairs of Jabba the Hutt's desert palace and his estate in Mos Eisley. Before working with Jabba, Bib Fortuna became rich as a slave trader of his own people, the Twi'leks.

Lekku (head-tails; one of two)

Fortuna hovers near Jabba's ear, whispering advice. Secretly, he plots to kill Jabba!

Silver bracelet

Tricked

Bib Fortuna is the new overlord of Jabba the Hutt's criminal group on Tatooine. He lives an unhealthy lifestyle of inactivity and self-indulgence. He is surprised to learn Boba Fett is alive and has come to visit him.

Traditional Ryloth robe

BIB FORTUNA

is a powerful and dreaded individual in Jabba's entourage. Whether you are a friend or a foe, Fortuna will use underhand means against you in order to maintain his control within the organization.

BISTAN

U-WING DOOR GUNNER

DATA FILE

AFFILIATION: Rebel Alliance
HOMEWORLD: Iakaru
SPECIES: Iakaru
HEIGHT: 1.73m (5ft 8in)
APPEARANCES: RO
SEE ALSO: Pao

Orange eye

BISTAN IS A CORPORAL in the Rebel Alliance Special Forces. He flies with Blue Squadron at the Battle of Scarif, firing his door-mounted ion blaster. Bistan is a ferocious enemy to have, but a fun and sociable squadmate.

Spacesuit sealing ring

THE IAKARU evolved to live in trees, so Bistan has good balance for perching on the ledge of a speeding U-wing. Life in the jungle canopy has also given him keen eyesight, excellent depth perception, and quick reflexes.

On Iakaru, Bistan fought with rocks and spears, but he takes to modern weapons with zeal.

Strength in Numbers

Bistan fled Iakaru when it was overrun by the Empire. Its lush rainforests, full of medicinal plants, are now being plundered by pharmaceutical companies. The best way Bistan can fight for his planet is with the Rebel Alliance.

BO-KATAN KRYZE

MANDALORIAN HEIRESS AND WARRIOR

DATA FILE

AFFILIATION: Mandalorians
HOMEWORLD: Mandalore
SPECIES: Human
HEIGHT: 1.8m (5ft 11in)
APPEARANCES: M
SEE ALSO: Axe Woves;
Koska Reeves;
the Mandalorian

Nite Owl helmet

Moff Gideon appears to relish how Mando's ownership of the Darksaber upsets her plans.

Belt pouches contain useful equipment

BO-KATAN KRYZE was the rightful leader of Mandalore, but lost her title due to the rise of the Empire. She searches the galaxy for Moff Gideon to reclaim the legendary Darksaber so she can use the blade to once again regain her position as Mandalore's leader.

WESTAR-35 blaster pistol

DURING THE Clone Wars, Bo-Katan clashes with her pacifist sister, Duchess Satine Kryze, ruler of Mandalore. When Satine is murdered by former Sith Lord Maul, Bo-Katan redirects her energy into taking on the Empire and securing a new future for her people.

Travel boots

Warrior Dilemma

Bo-Katan joins the Mandalorian's mission to rescue Grogu from Moff Gideon, hoping to claim the Darksaber for herself. After an epic battle, Din Djarin takes the weapon from Moff Gideon. He offers it to Bo-Katan, but she declines because she did not win it in combat.

BOBA FETT

THE BEST BOUNTY HUNTER IN THE GALAXY

DATA FILE

AFFILIATION: Bounty hunter
HOMEWORLD: Kamino
SPECIES: Human (clone)
HEIGHT: 1.83m (6ft)
APPEARANCES: II, IV, V, VI, M
SEE ALSO: Darth Vader;
Han Solo; Jabba the Hutt;
Jango Fett; The Mandalorian

COOL AND CALCULATING, Boba Fett is a legendary bounty hunter and one of the most dangerous killers in the galaxy. He lives by an unknown code of honor and only accepts missions that serve his purpose. Boba Fett's enemies rarely survive an encounter with him.

Multifunction helmet

Reinforced flight suit

BOBA FETT'S talent and skill, combined with an arsenal of exotic weapons, have brought in many "impossible" bounties. He is notorious for completely disintegrating those whom he has been hired to track down.

Boba is hired to track down the *Millennium Falcon* after the Battle of Hoth, which leads him to Cloud City, located in the upper atmosphere of the gas giant Bespin.

EE-3 blaster rifle

On the Hunt

Boba Fett spends years looking for his missing armor, which originally belonged to his father, Jango Fett, and is presumed buried in the stomach of a Sarlacc on Tatooine. He watches the Mandalorian speed away with it and is determined to be reunited with his family's legacy.

Working for Darth Vader, Fett captures Han Solo and loads his carbon-frozen body into his ship.

BOBBAJO

CRITTERMONGER AND STORYTELLER

SHUFFLING HIS rare animal merchandise to various marketplaces and trading posts is Bobbajo, known to many simply as the Crittermonger. He is also known as the Storyteller, for his habit of spinning long and unlikely yarns.

Sneep

Head wrapping

Long, flexible neck

THE CREAKY-JOINTED
Nu-Cosian has an unflappable, kind personality that has a calming effect on the jittery creatures he keeps in his cages. It also lends a magical quality to his storytelling, as his gentle nature attracts many listeners.

Old Wanderer

Bobbajo has been a fixture on Jakku and nearby worlds for decades. To ensure he always has exotic merchandise, he braves the most treacherous terrain, including the crumbling cliffs of Carbon Ridge. He trudges through the shifting landscape as if following his own peculiar rhythm, ignoring the many dangers that surround him.

BODHI ROOK

IMPERIAL DEFECTOR

Flight goggles

Weatherproof poncho for Eadu's wet climate

Imperial flight suit

BODHI ROOK was an ordinary pilot flying cargo for the Empire. One day he is given a message that could change the course of the galaxy. It turns him into an Imperial deserter, a wanted man—and a rebel hero.

WHEN BODHI wasn't ferrying kyber crystals from Jedha to the Imperial research facility on Eadu, he gambled on odupiendo races. Watching these super-fast running birds honed his piloting skills, giving him an eye for speed and tactics.

Piloting Rogue One, a name he came up with, Bodhi gains clearance to pass through the shield gate at Scarif.

Brave Messenger

Delivering Galen Erso's message to the rebels is not easy. Finding Saw Gerrera without being killed is hard enough for Bodhi, but convincing him of the truth is impossible. Deeply suspicious, Gerrera interrogates Bodhi with help from a terrifying Mairan, Bor Gullet, and then locks him up. Bodhi finds he is more courageous than he thought.

BOOLIO

RESISTANCE SPY

DATA FILE

AFFILIATION: Resistance
HOMEWORLD: Sinta IV
SPECIES: Ovissian
HEIGHT: 1.78m (5ft 10in)
APPEARANCES: IX
SEE ALSO: Finn; Kylo Ren

Ovissians have four horns

BOOLIO WORKS as a mine overseer at the Sinta Glacier Colony. He shares data with the Resistance that suggests there is a spy in the First Order.

Location data recorder

Filament wire warms suit

After helping the Resistance, Boolio is arrested by the First Order and brought before Supreme Leader Kylo Ren.

BOOLIO USES his sense of humor and positive attitude to keep his workers' spirits up on the ice glacier they call home. Despite the risk of being caught by the First Order, Boolio finds ways to funnel resources and information to the Resistance as often as he can.

Risky Transmission

Boolio refuses payment for his work with the Resistance, as he has a high regard for General Organa and her ongoing efforts to defeat the First Order. He insists all intelligence be communicated face to face, even though patrols have increased at the Sinta Colony.

BOSS NASS

GUNGAN LEADER

DATA FILE

AFFILIATION: Gungan High Council; Gungan Grand Army
HOMEWORLD: Naboo
SPECIES: Gungan
HEIGHT: 2.06m (6ft 9in)
APPEARANCES: I, III
SEE ALSO: Jar Jar Binks; Padmé Amidala

Crown of rulership

Epaulets of military authority

Four-fingered hand

The Gungan High Council has the power to summon the Gungan Grand Army.

BOSS NASS

sits on the Gungan High Council. He is a fair but stubborn ruler. He particularly resents the Naboo's belief that the Gungans are primitive simply because Gungans prefer to use traditional crafts and technologies.

Long coat with golden clasp

BOSS NASS is the stern, old-fashioned ruler of Otoh Gunga, the largest of the Gungan underwater cities on Naboo. He speaks Galactic Basic (the most widely used language in the galaxy) with a strong accent.

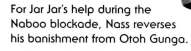

For Jar Jar's help during the Naboo blockade, Nass reverses his banishment from Otoh Gunga.

Teamwork

When his planet is faced with invasion, Boss Nass puts aside his prejudice against the Naboo. He receives Queen Amidala when she humbly asks him for help. Boss Nass realizes that his people must work together with the Naboo or die, and a new friendship is forged between the two cultures.

BOSSK

TRANDOSHAN BOUNTY HUNTER

DATA FILE

AFFILIATION: Bounty hunter
HOMEWORLD: Trandosha
SPECIES: Trandoshan
HEIGHT: 1.9m (6ft 2in)
APPEARANCES: V, VI
SEE ALSO: Aurra Sing;
Boba Fett; Darth Vader

Eyes can see in infrared range

THE TOUGH AND RESILIENT Bossk is a reptilian Trandoshan bounty hunter. He pilots a ship named the *Hound's Tooth*, claims bounties for the right price, and is incredibly successful at capturing his prey.

Sling for grenade launcher

Flak vest

Relby v-10 micro grenade launcher

BOSSK began his career doing a form of bounty hunting that few other species would risk: hunting Wookiees. Later, he hunts other species. During the Clone Wars, Bossk teams up with Aurra Sing, young Boba Fett, and a Klatooinian bounty hunter named Castas.

Lost fingers, skin, and even limbs can regrow until adulthood

Bossk and other bounty hunters frequently visit Jabba the Hutt, seeking their next job.

Tough Trandoshan

Fond of skinning his captives when possible, Bossk is as vile and mean as they come. He is one of the six bounty hunters Darth Vader enlists to track down and capture the *Millennium Falcon*.

BOUSHH

DATA FILE

AFFILIATION: Bounty hunter
HOMEWORLD: Uba IV
SPECIES: Ubese
HEIGHT: 1.5m (4ft 9in)
APPEARANCES: VI
SEE ALSO: Chewbacca;
Jabba the Hutt;
Princess Leia

Speech scrambler

Glove spikes

Projectile detonator

THE GALAXY contains many bizarre creatures acting as bounty hunters (or claiming to be). Princess Leia adopts a convincing identity as an Ubese tracker, Boushh, to gain entry to Jabba's palace. Only Jabba suspects her identity is false.

Shata leather pants

Leia, in disguise as Boushh, prepares to release Han Solo from frozen captivity.

BOUSHH battles Leia on Ord Mantell, where Leia travels seeking help to free Han Solo from carbonite. Maz Kanata helps Leia defeat Boushh so Leia can use his armor and helmet as a disguise to fool Jabba the Hutt.

Ammo pouch

Jabba's suspicions prove correct as he catches Leia unmasked with Han.

Traditional Ubese boots

Boushh's Bounty

At Jabba's palace, Chewbacca pretends to be Boushh's captive, and Boushh demands a high price for the captured Wookiee. When Jabba disagrees over the amount of credits, Boushh pulls out a thermal detonator.

BURG

DEVARONIAN MERCENARY

DATA FILE

AFFILIATION: Ranzar Malk's crew
HOMEWORLD: Devaron
SPECIES: Devaronian
HEIGHT: 1.9m (6ft 3in)
APPEARANCES M
SEE ALSO: Migs Mayfeld; Q9-0; Ranzar Malk; Xi'an

BRASH BURG is part of Ranzar Malk's criminal crew. Malk describes Burg as "the muscle"—a title Burg is happy to demonstrate during missions. Burg isn't impressed with the Mandalorian, Din Djarin, and questions why he was added to their crew.

Blaster pistol

Leather holsters hold twin blasters

TO MATCH his aggressive personality, Burg's main forms of communication are grunts and growls. Like all male Devaronians, Burg's head is topped with two fierce-looking horns, formed from bone. Their appearance and temperament combined make them well suited to a life of crime.

Coat split for ease of movement

Brute Strength

Burg is incredibly strong, even for a Devaronian, but he is not very strategic. His first instinct when he runs into a new enemy is to rush at it, blast it, or destroy it—even when those around him dash for cover. He also has a cruel sense of humor and will often belittle those he sees as beneath him.

Burg doesn't trust Xi'an, but he respects her knife skills and her ruthlessness during jobs.

Double-layered boots

C-3PO

GOLDEN PROTOCOL DROID

DATA FILE

AFFILIATION: Republic; Rebel Alliance; Resistance
TYPE: Protocol droid
MANUFACTURER: Cybot Galactica
HEIGHT: 1.67m (5ft 6in)
APPEARANCES: I, II, III, RO, IV, V, VI, VII, VIII, IX
SEE ALSO: Anakin Skywalker; Luke Skywalker; R2-D2

Vocabulator

C-3PO IS PROGRAMMED to assist in matters of etiquette and translation. Thrown into a world of adventure, he is often overwhelmed by the action around him. But he forms a capable team when partnered with the resourceful R2-D2.

Bronzium finish polished to a dazzling shine

Primary power coupling outlet

Following surgery on Kijimi, C-3PO awakens with red eyes.

Reinforced knee joint

C-3PO first works for Anakin Skywalker and his mother, Shmi. Anakin then gives C-3PO to Senator Padmé Amidala as a wedding gift. After Padmé's death, C-3PO is assigned to Bail Organa, until Darth Vader captures the *Tantive IV*. C-3PO escapes to Tatooine and is sold to Luke Skywalker.

Golden God
Despite his fear of excitement, C-3PO has led an adventurous life, often losing limbs or bits of circuitry along the way (though he is easily repaired). On Endor, a tribe of Ewoks worships C-3PO as a "golden god," which leads the Ewoks to support the rebels and play a decisive role in defeating the Empire.

C'AI THRENALLI

HOTSHOT PILOT

DATA FILE

AFFILIATION: Resistance
HOMEWORLD: Abednedo
SPECIES: Abednedo
HEIGHT: 1.88m (6ft 2in)
APPEARANCES: VII, VIII, IX
SEE ALSO: Lieutenant Connix; Poe Dameron

Dangling mouth tentacles

C'AI THRENALLI is Poe Dameron's wingman in the Resistance Starfighter Corps. As comfortable flying an X-wing starfighter as much as a regular airspeeder, he can turn his hand to any controls.

C'ai Threnalli is an Abednedo like Ello Asty, one of the pilots who helped to destroy Starkiller Base.

MANY ABEDNEDO

have integrated into life across the galaxy. They mix well with other species thanks to their sociability, intelligence, and curiosity. In his orange flight suit, C'ai blends in with the rest of the rebel pilots, except for his specially shaped helmet.

Lucky Survivor

C'ai is loyal to Poe Dameron and sides with him in his mutiny against Vice Admiral Holdo. However, in the end, C'ai survives the D'Qar evacuation thanks to Holdo's plan and her self-sacrifice. He is also one of the few rebels who live to tell the tale of the Battle of Crait.

Feet have three toes

Signal flares

CANTO BIGHT POLICE

CORRUPT OFFICERS OF THE LAW

DATA FILE

AFFILIATION: Canto Bight Police Department
HOMEWORLD: Varies
SPECIES: Human
HEIGHT (AVG.): 1.83m (6ft)
STANDARD EQUIPMENT: K-25 blaster; stun prod
APPEARANCES: VIII
SEE ALSO: Finn; Rose Tico

THE CANTO BIGHT Police Department maintains order in the casino-city on Cantonica. However, it concerns itself more with appearances than with its poorer citizens. Its priority is the rich visitors: if they feel safe and valued, then they will keep spending.

Mirror-image lettering

Flexible betaplast neck guard

Betaplast armored collar

POLICE uniforms are designed to give guests reassurance, while also being equipped for swift, discreet action against anyone who disturbs the peace. Officers do not want an ugly scene to damage the city's reputation.

The police headquarters and surveillance building sits on a hill near Canto Bight, overlooking the city.

Iniquity

Penalties are high for anyone who disrupts Canto Bight's lavishly maintained public areas—like Rose Tico and Finn who park their shuttle on a beach. However, more serious crime can be overlooked—if you're rich enough to bribe the police.

Electro-shock stun prod

CAPTAIN ANTILLES

CAPTAIN OF THE *TANTIVE IV*

DATA FILE

AFFILIATION: Republic; Rebel Alliance
HOMEWORLD: Alderaan
SPECIES: Human
HEIGHT: 1.88m (6ft 2in)
APPEARANCES: III, IV, RO
SEE ALSO: Bail Organa; Princess Leia

CAPTAIN ANTILLES is a highly capable pilot. He has taken part in many daring missions for the rebels, and has had notable success breaking through Imperial blockades.

Target blaster

CAPTAIN RAYMUS ANTILLES is commander of Bail Organa's fleet of diplomatic cruisers. During the Imperial era, Antilles becomes a rebel and serves as captain of the *Tantive IV* under Organa's adopted daughter, Leia Organa.

Cape of Alderaanian nobility

Wrist guard

The Alderaan royal family owns the diplomatic cruiser *Tantive IV*.

Flight boots

Stranglehold

In the battle over Tatooine, Darth Vader boards the *Tantive IV* and demands that Antilles surrenders the stolen Death Star plans. When he refuses, Vader destroys him.

CAPTAIN ITHANO

CRIMSON CORSAIR

DATA FILE

AFFILIATION: None
HOMEWORLD: Unknown
SPECIES: Delphidian
HEIGHT: 1.93m (6ft 4in)
APPEARANCES: VII, IX
SEE ALSO: Finn;
Maz Kanata

THE ERA OF LAWLESSNESS that follows the Galactic Civil War leads to the rise of the colorful pirate Sidon Ithano. Ithano uses many flashy aliases, and tales of his exploits continue to grow.

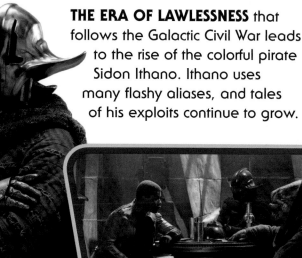

Captured Kanjiklub rifle

Ithano's polished Kaleesh war helmet conceals his Delphidian features.

Pirate Crew

Ithano pilots the *Meson Martinet*, and his pirate crew (which includes his one-legged First Mate Quiggold) runs a smooth ship. Finn very nearly joins Ithano's crew at Maz's castle, when he tries to find a new life after deserting from the First Order.

Armorweave-lined cape

ITHANO IS
extremely vain, and relishes stories of his deeds as the "Blood Buccaneer," the "Crimson Corsair," or the "Red Raider." He lets these stories do the hard work for him, as many targeted vessels surrender without putting up a fight.

CAPTAIN LANG

MORGAN ELSBETH'S ENFORCER

DATA FILE

AFFILIATION: Magistrate Morgan Elsbeth
HOMEWORLD: Corvus
SPECIES: Human
HEIGHT: 1.83m (6ft)
APPEARANCES: M
SEE ALSO: Ahsoka Tano; The Mandalorian; Morgan Elsbeth

Non-standard military pauldron

Hiring Din Djarin

Morgan Elsbeth wants to destroy former Jedi Knight Ahsoka Tano, but Captain Lang and his forces have so far proved no match for Ahsoka and her lightsabers. Elsbeth hires the Mandalorian, Din Djarin, in the hope that he will succeed where Lang has failed.

CAPTAIN LANG serves Morgan Elsbeth as the magistrate's captain of the guard on the planet Corvus. Cruel and corrupt, he is loyal to Elsbeth only because she pays him well. Lang is well-trained and quick with a blaster.

Buckle with communications device

Leather holster

CAPTAIN LANG is a dangerous gun for hire who the Mandalorian thinks may have previously belonged to a military group. Lang defends Morgan Elsbeth's walled city, Calodan, from outsiders and helps enforce her cold-blooded treatment of prisoners.

Lang respects the Mandalorian but doubts he can defeat Tano.

CAPTAIN NEEDA

COMMANDER OF THE *AVENGER*

DATA FILE

AFFILIATION: Empire
HOMEWORLD: Coruscant
SPECIES: Human
HEIGHT: 1.75m (5ft 9in)
APPEARANCES: V
SEE ALSO: Admiral Ozzel;
Darth Vader

CAPTAIN NEEDA IS COMMANDER of the Imperial Star Destroyer *Avenger*, which takes part in the search for the rebels' hidden bases. Needa follows the *Falcon* into an asteroid field and back out, but then loses the ship completely.

Standard-issue
officer's gloves

Imperial officer's tunic

Belt buckle with
data storage

LORTH NEEDA is a dependable and ruthless officer who served the Galactic Republic in the Clone Wars during the Battle of Coruscant, when General Grievous "kidnapped" Chancellor Palpatine. Now an Imperial officer, Needa fails to live up to Darth Vader's exacting standards.

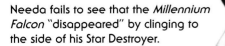

Needa fails to see that the *Millennium Falcon* "disappeared" by clinging to the side of his Star Destroyer.

No Mercy

When Needa loses sight of the *Falcon*, he apologizes to Vader, accepting full responsibility. Vader accepts Needa's apology—then Force-chokes him.

CAPTAIN PANAKA

NABOO HEAD OF SECURITY

DATA FILE

AFFILIATION: Naboo Royal Security Forces
HOMEWORLD: Naboo
SPECIES: Human
HEIGHT: 1.83m (6ft)
APPEARANCES: I
SEE ALSO: Padmé Amidala

AS HEAD OF SECURITY for Queen Amidala on Naboo, Captain Quarsh Panaka oversees every branch of the volunteer Naboo Royal Security Forces. During the invasion of Naboo, Panaka sees the dangerous state of affairs in the galaxy and argues for stronger security.

Leather jerkin

Utility belt

CAPTAIN PANAKA

gained combat experience in a Republic Special Task Force, fighting against space pilots in the sector containing the Naboo system.

High officer headgear

Stripes on coat indicate rank

After Queen Amidala's abdication, Panaka serves Queen Jamillia.

Royal Responsibility

Panaka is responsible for Queen Amidala's safety, accompanying her during the escape from Naboo. When the queen returns to Naboo to reclaim her throne, Panaka is by her side, offering cover fire during the infiltration of the palace.

CAPTAIN PHASMA

STORMTROOPER COMMANDER

DATA FILE

AFFILIATION: First Order
HOMEWORLD: Parnassos
SPECIES: Human
HEIGHT (IN ARMOR):
2m (6ft 7in)
APPEARANCES: VII, VIII
SEE ALSO: Finn; First Order
stormtrooper; General Hux;
Kylo Ren

CLAD IN DISTINCTIVE metallic armor, Captain Phasma commands the First Order's legions of stormtroopers. She sees it as her duty to ensure only the best soldiers serve the First Order.

Chromium-plated
F-11D blaster rifle

Crush gauntlets

Armorweave cape

When FN-2187, a stormtrooper under her command, abandons his duties and defects to the Resistance, Phasma takes it as a personal failing.

DESPITE HER RANK,
Phasma prefers combat to administrative work. She carries a personalized F-11D blaster rifle alongside the more commonly seen blaster pistol. Her armor is coated in salvaged chromium that makes her stand out and emphasizes her authority.

Forged in Battle

Phasma believes that true soldiers are only made in combat. Though she recognizes the value of the complex simulations used in stormtrooper training, she thinks that success in simulations is no real guarantee of a soldier's bravery.

CAPTAIN SABROND

SITH ETERNAL OFFICER

DATA FILE

AFFILIATION: Final Order; Sith Eternal
HOMEWORLD: Exegol
SPECIES: Human
HEIGHT: 1.62m (5ft 4in)
APPEARANCES: IX
SEE ALSO: General Pryde; Palpatine

Sith Eternal crest

RAISED BY Sith Eternal cultists on Exegol, Captain Chesille Sabrond believes she is part of an army destined to rule the galaxy. Her Final Order Star Destroyer, the *Derriphan*, is equipped with a superlaser capable of destroying an entire planet.

Single red stripe denotes officer rank

SABROND'S RUTHLESSNESS and lifelong devotion to the Sith is rewarded when she is ordered to leave Exegol to destroy the planet Kijimi. This deadly act is the first display of power in Palpatine's Final Order plans.

Pants securely tucked into boots

True Believer

Sith Eternal officers like Sabrond spend their lives secretly training on Exegol in a devoted attempt to return the Sith to power. The fleet is kept a secret from both the Resistance and the First Order for many years.

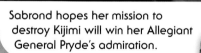

Sabrond hopes her mission to destroy Kijimi will win her Allegiant General Pryde's admiration.

Slip-resistant boots

CAPTAIN TYPHO

SENATOR AMIDALA'S HEAD OF SECURITY

DATA FILE

AFFILIATION: Naboo Royal Security Forces
HOMEWORLD: Naboo
SPECIES: Human
HEIGHT: 1.85m (6ft 1in)
APPEARANCES: II, III
SEE ALSO: Captain Panaka; Padmé Amidala

Naboo royal uniform

Eye lost during Battle of Naboo

CAPTAIN TYPHO is well respected for his loyalty. His uncle, Captain Panaka, was head of security for Padmé Amidala when she was Queen of Naboo. Now Typho oversees security for Padmé in her role as senator for Naboo.

Synthetic leather gauntlets

Naboo blaster

AT THE TIME of the Battle of Naboo, Typho was a Junior Palace Guard. Despite his young age, Typho played a brave part in the conflict, losing his eye in the line of duty. Captain Typho is given his Senatorial post because of his loyalty and his ties to Panaka.

Captain Typho is by Amidala's side on many missions throughout the Clone Wars.

A Dangerous World

Captain Typho accompanies Senator Amidala to Coruscant, where an assassination attempt kills seven in his command, including Padmé's handmaiden Cordé (disguised as Padmé). Typho soon realizes that even his strict security measures might not be enough in the new, dangerous world of the Clone Wars.

CARA DUNE

MARSHAL OF NEVARRO

AFFILIATION: Rebel Alliance; New Republic
HOMEWORLD: Alderaan
SPECIES: Human
HEIGHT: 1.73m (5ft 8in)
APPEARANCES: M
SEE ALSO: Greef Karga; Grogu; the Mandalorian

Rebel starbird tear tattoo

CARA DUNE WAS a rebel dropper from Alderaan and is a veteran of the Galactic Civil War. Now she helps keep the peace as the marshal of Nevarro. Not one to shy away from danger, Cara is loyal to her friends and hates the Empire.

Shock trooper pauldron

Light repeating blaster rifle

AFTER THE fall of the Empire, Cara Dune becomes a soldier for hire and lives alone on the planet Sorgan. She decides to fight for a greater cause when she meets the Mandalorian and Grogu.

Dropper armor piece

Cara tells Captain Carson Teva that she lost everyone when the Death Star destroyed Alderaan.

The Winner Is...

Cara Dune is a superior brawler—and a smart, highly skilled fighter. She makes money on Sorgan fighting against opponents who are often much bigger than her. She is not easy to intimidate and rarely loses.

Synthleather boots

CARDO

KNIGHT OF REN ARMORER

DATA FILE

AFFILIATION: Knights of Ren
HOMEWORLD: Unknown
SPECIES: Unknown
HEIGHT: 1.75m
(5ft 9in)
APPEARANCES:
VII, IX
SEE ALSO: Ap'lek;
Kuruk; Kylo Ren;
Trudgen; Ushar;
Vicrul

Customized helmet

Modified arm cannon

Cardo and the other Knights follow Rey and her Resistance allies to the desert world of Pasaana.

CARDO IS obsessed with modifying weapons, which he supplies to the other Knights. His own weapon of choice is a cannon that can also launch plasma bolts and jets of burning flame.

THE KNIGHTS of Ren answer only to their leader, Kylo Ren. Many officers in the First Order, including General Hux, despise the filthy presence of the ghoul-like Knights of Ren in the polished corridors of their spotless capital ships.

Flame resistant coat

Armored greaves

On the Hunt

The Knights of Ren search for any signs of Rey on the cold, mountainous planet of Kijimi. The Knights regularly work together as a pack to increase their chances of outnumbering and intimidating any opposition.

CARSON TEVA

NEW REPUBLIC CAPTAIN AND PILOT

DATA FILE

AFFILIATION: Rebel Alliance; New Republic
HOMEWORLD: Unknown
SPECIES: Human
HEIGHT: 1.75m (5ft 9in)
APPEARANCES: M
SEE ALSO: Cara Dune; the Mandalorian

New Republic symbol

CAPTAIN CARSON TEVA is a pilot in the New Republic. He is an honorable man who is highly respected by his peers. He invites Cara Dune to join him in helping to remove the Imperial Remnant from the Outer Rim Territories.

A280 Blaster rifle and scope

CARSON believes in the New Republic. He trusts people who, like him, are dedicated to stopping Imperials from harming others. He is aware that the Mandalorian has worked with criminals in the past, but does not arrest him because he knows Mando has also done a lot of good.

Orange flight suit

Captain Carson Teva flies an X-wing for the New Republic and is an excellent pilot.

Questioning the Magistrate

Carson Teva goes to Nevarro to find out about a recent explosion at an abandoned Imperial base. He also wants to find out if the Magistrate Greef Karga has seen the Mandalorian lately.

Synthleather reinforced pilot boots

CASSIAN ANDOR

REBEL INTELLIGENCE AGENT

DATA FILE

AFFILIATION: Rebel Alliance; Rogue One
HOMEWORLD: Fest
SPECIES: Human
HEIGHT: 1.78m (5ft 10in)
APPEARANCES: RO
SEE ALSO: Jyn Erso; K-2SO

CAPTAIN CASSIAN ANDOR lives and breathes the Rebel Alliance. His role in military intelligence often puts him on the front line, gathering snippets of information that could be used against the Empire. He goes by many names and blends into a crowd.

Captain's pips

Corellian-style field jacket

BlasTech A280-CFE weapon

CASSIAN JERON Andor

has been caught up in violence since he was six years old. His traumatic experiences and aimless early years have focused his determination to disrupt the Empire. He fights it with whatever minor acts of rebellion he can, hoping that it will all one day amount to a greater effect.

Cassian is able to call on a network of informants across the galaxy for intelligence vital to the rebel cause.

Going Rogue

For an intelligence officer, there is no greater prize than the files of the Death Star. Stealing them from under the Empire's nose means going on a suicide mission, against orders. But the data gets through: mission complete.

CHANCELLOR VALORUM

HEAD OF THE REPUBLIC BEFORE PALPATINE

BEFORE PALPATINE becomes Supreme Chancellor, Finis Valorum holds the highest position in the Galactic Senate. He rules the Republic when Trade Federation warships blockade the peaceful planet of Naboo. Padmé Amidala blames Valorum personally.

Ornate overcloak

Blue band symbolic of Supreme Chancellor

When Valorum resigns, Senator Palpatine steps in, promising strength and effectiveness.

Veda cloth robe

VALORUM comes from a family of politicians. All his life, he has been preparing for the office of Supreme Chancellor. This is a man who enjoys the privileges of a head of state. However, this attitude does not endear him to ordinary voters.

Weak Leader

While Naboo suffers, the Senate debates its options, but does not act. The Speaker, Mas Amedda (secretly working for Palpatine), knows that this indecision will make Valorum look weak and ineffective.

CHEWBACCA

WOOKIEE WARRIOR, PILOT, AND HERO

DATA FILE

AFFILIATION: Rebel Alliance; Resistance
HOMEWORLD: Kashyyyk
SPECIES: Wookiee
HEIGHT: 2.28m (7ft 6in)
APPEARANCES: III, S, IV, V, VI, VII, VIII, IX
SEE ALSO: Han Solo; Tarfful

CHEWBACCA is a Wookiee mechanic and pilot. During the Clone Wars, he fights to defend his planet. Under the Empire, he is first mate, mechanic, and loyal friend to Han Solo aboard the *Millennium Falcon*.

CHEWIE SERVES

as Han Solo's fiercely loyal copilot and trusty fellow adventurer. He enjoys the thrilling action that Solo gets them into, but sometimes tries to act as a check on his partner's willfulness.

Bowcaster

Water-shedding hair

Tool pouch

Thirty years after the Rebel Alliance, Han and Chewie are still side by side.

Unlikely Friendship

Chewbacca first meets Han Solo in an Imperial prison pit on Mimban, and they get off to a violent start. Han is supposed to be Chewie's dinner, but he manages to escape and takes the Wookiee along for the ride.

CHIEF CHIRPA

EWOK LEADER

WISE CHIEF CHIRPA has led the Bright Tree tribe on the forest moon of Endor for 42 seasons. When his Ewok tribe captures a Rebel Alliance strike force, Chirpa is only stopped from sacrificing them by C-3PO, whom the superstitious Ewoks believe is a "golden god."

Hood

Acute sense of smell

Chief's medallion

Reptilian staff

CHIEF Chirpa leads his village with understanding, though he has become a bit forgetful in his old age. His authority commits the Ewoks to their dangerous fight against the Empire.

Hunting knife

The Bright Tree tribe lives in a village high up in the treetops.

New Recruits

After listening to C-3PO's account of the resistance to the Empire, Chirpa commits the Ewoks to the struggle. In the Battle of Endor, the Ewok warriors use all their cunning and fierceness to defeat the superior forces of the Imperial Army.

CHIRRUT ÎMWE

GUARDIAN OF THE WHILLS

DATA FILE

AFFILIATION: Guardian of the Whills (former)
HOMEWORLD: Jedha
SPECIES: Human
HEIGHT: 1.73m (5ft 8in)
APPEARANCES: RO
SEE ALSO: Baze Malbus; Bodhi Rook; Cassian Andor; Jyn Erso; K-2SO

WITH INTENSE TRAINING and focus, Chirrut Îmwe has turned his body into a skilled fighting machine. Îmwe is intensely spiritual and believes deeply in the Force. His lack of eyesight does not stop him from being a formidable warrior.

Gauntlet for steadying lightbow shots

Lightbow slung over shoulder

Staff made of uneti wood

AS GUARDIAN of the Whills, Îmwe belongs to an ancient order of warrior monks. Its main role is to protect the Temple of the Kyber in the Holy City of Jedha. This sacred job becomes obsolete when the whole city is destroyed by a single test shot from the Death Star.

Ancient kasaya robes

Îmwe knocks down stormtroopers with elegant but deadly twirls of his uneti-wood staff.

Warrior Monk

Muttering mantras gives Îmwe strength to face the enemy against terrible odds. He is a master of the martial art zama-shiwo, so he can achieve a peaceful mental and physical state. He gains control over his body, even his heart rate and oxygen intake. He adopts this practice at the Battle of Scarif.

CLIEGG LARS

SHMI SKYWALKER'S HUSBAND

DATA FILE

AFFILIATION: None
HOMEWORLD: Tatooine
SPECIES: Human
HEIGHT: 1.83m (6ft)
APPEARANCES: II
SEE ALSO: Beru Lars; Owen Lars; Shmi Skywalker

WHEN TATOOINE moisture farmer Cliegg Lars goes looking for a farmhand in Mos Espa, he instead meets and falls in love with Shmi Skywalker, Anakin Skywalker's mother. In order to marry Shmi, Cliegg buys her freedom from Watto, the flying junk dealer who keeps her in enslavement.

Gear harness

Weather-worn work clothes

Cliegg loses a leg in his attempt to rescue Shmi from Tusken Raiders.

CLIEGG'S father was a Tatooinian farmer, but young Cliegg wanted to experience life on a bustling Core World. Here, he fell in love with and married Aika. But when Aika died, Cliegg returned to Tatooine to run the family farm.

Heartbroken

Cliegg loses Shmi when Tusken Raiders kidnap and kill her. After her death, Cliegg remains determined to live the life he has worked so hard to create. Sadly, he dies shortly afterward from a broken heart.

THE CLIENT

DATA FILE

AFFILIATION: Empire; Imperial Remnant
HOMEWORLD: Unknown
SPECIES: Human
HEIGHT: 1.83m (6ft)
APPEARANCES: M
SEE ALSO: Doctor Pershing; the Mandalorian; Moff Gideon

The Client and Doctor Pershing examine Grogu to make sure he is fit for their experiments.

THE OTHERWISE nameless Client hires the Mandalorian to locate an unknown prize that is important to the Imperial Remnant. He is polite and softly spoken but is deadly serious about his plans for this so-called asset.

Fur-edged coat

Imperial sigil indicating high honor

Tracking fob for the asset

ALTHOUGH the Imperial era is over, the Client looks back at those times fondly and still wears an Imperial medallion. He is obsessed with finding the child named Grogu for his superior, Moff Gideon.

Return to Glory

The Client hires the Mandalorian, even though he is expensive, because of his reputation as the best in the parsec. He gives Mando a large amount of beskar and tells him this will begin to make up for the Empire's destruction of Mandalore.

CLONE PILOT

SPECIALIST CLONE AIRMEN

DATA FILE

AFFILIATION: Republic; Empire
HOMEWORLD: Kamino
SPECIES: Human (clone)
HEIGHT: 1.83m (6ft)
STANDARD EQUIPMENT: DC-15A blaster; thermal detonators; ammunition
APPEARANCES: II, III
SEE ALSO: Clone trooper

Anti-glare blast visor

Air-supply hose

CLONE PILOTS are cross-trained to fly a wide variety of combat craft in service to the Republic. These skilled soldiers can pilot LAAT gunships, Y-wing bombers, ARC-170 fighters, and V-wing fighters.

Rebreather unit

A pilot and copilot/forward gunner fly an ARC-170 fighter at the Battle of Coruscant.

Flight data records pouch

IN THE BATTLE OF

Coruscant, most clone pilots wear Phase II pilot armor, with helmets fitted with anti-glare blast visors. V-wing pilots, however, wear fully enclosed helmets since these ships carry no onboard life-support systems.

Gunship Pilots

At the start of the Clone Wars, in the Battle of Geonosis, clone pilots fly LAAT/i and LAAT/c gunships. They wear Phase I battle armor, distinguished by yellow markings and specialized full-face helmets.

CLONE TROOPER (PHASE I)

DATA FILE

AFFILIATION: Republic
HOMEWORLD: Kamino
SPECIES: Human (clone)
HEIGHT: 1.83m (6ft)
STANDARD EQUIPMENT: DC-15 blaster; thermal detonators; ammunition
APPEARANCES: II
SEE ALSO: Clone trooper (Phase II); clone pilot; Jango Fett

Breath filter

Clone troopers are deployed from Republic assault ships, which also carry gunships.

DC-15 blaster

Utility belt

Thigh plate

THE FIRST CLONE troopers are designated Phase I because of their style of armor. Born and raised in Kaminoan cloning factories, they are trained for no other purpose than to fight, and feel virtually invincible.

PHASE I armor is loosely based on Jango Fett's Mandalorian armor. It consists of 20 armor plates and is often referred to as the "body bucket" because it is heavy and uncomfortable.

High-traction soles

First Strike

When the Separatist droid army makes its first all-out strike on Geonosis, the Senate has no choice but to send in an army of clone soldiers that it has neither amassed nor trained. Under the skillful command of the Jedi, the clones force a droid retreat.

CLONE TROOPER (PHASE II)

SECOND GENERATION CLONE TROOPERS

DATA FILE

AFFILIATION: Republic; Empire
HOMEWORLD: Kamino
SPECIES: Human (clone)
HEIGHT: 1.83m (6ft)
STANDARD EQUIPMENT:
DC-15A blaster; thermal
detonators; ammunition
APPEARANCES: III
SEE ALSO: Clone
trooper (Phase I)

Clone troopers form the galaxy's
best military force.

Battle-damaged
chest plastron

Spare
blaster magazine

Standard
DC-15A blaster
has a folding
stock

BY THE TIME of the
Battle of Coruscant,
clone troopers, with
enhanced Phase II
armor, are battle-dented
and mud-smeared. Aging
at twice the rate of
normally birthed humans,
only two-thirds of the
original army of clone
troopers are alive.

Knee
plate

PHASE II armor
is stronger, lighter, and
more adaptable than
Phase I armor, and has
many specialist variations.

Superior Troopers
Clone troopers are equipped with
far more advanced armor and
air support than the Separatists,
allowing them to easily cut
through the battle droid ranks.

COBB VANTH

MARSHAL OF MOS PELGO

DATA FILE

AFFILIATION: Mos Pelgo
HOMEWORLD: Tatooine
SPECIES: Human
HEIGHT: 1.83m (6ft)
APPEARANCES: M
SEE ALSO: The
Mandalorian;
Tusken Raider

Targeting rangefinder

COBB VANTH KEEPS the peace as the marshal of the small town of Mos Pelgo on Tatooine. He wears the armor of the legendary bounty hunter Boba Fett. Vanth later gives the armor to the Mandalorian in exchange for his help in defeating a deadly krayt dragon.

Helmet viewplate

Mandalorian jetpack

COBB VANTH is near death in the Tatooine desert when he is found by a group of Jawas. He discovers a full set of Mandalorian armor inside their sandcrawler and trades a box of silicax oxalate crystals for it.

Woodoo-leather holster

An Unlikely Team

The Mandalorian and Cobb Vanth work together to hunt down a krayt dragon, and are joined by a group of Tusken Raiders. Previously enemies, both sides realize they need each other to destroy the giant beast.

Mer-Sonn Munitions HF-94 heavy blaster pistol

Cobb Vanth enjoys a drink in the dark cantina on Mos Pelgo.

Kneepad dart launcher

COLEMAN TREBOR

VURK JEDI MASTER

DATA FILE

AFFILIATION: Jedi
HOMEWORLD: Sembla
SPECIES: Vurk
HEIGHT: 2.13m (7ft)
APPEARANCES: II
SEE ALSO: Count Dooku;
Yarael Poof

Bony head crest grows throughout life

Thick reptilian skin

Coleman Trebor joined the Jedi High Council after the death of Jedi Master Yarael Poof.

JEDI MASTER Coleman Trebor is revered as a skillful mediator, bringing difficult disputes to a harmonious end. His skill with a lightsaber is also impressive, and he joins Windu's taskforce to Geonosis.

Food and energy capsules

Jedi cloak

Facing Dooku

On Geonosis, Coleman Trebor seizes his opportunity and steps up to Count Dooku, taking the Separatist leader by surprise. But bounty hunter Jango Fett quickly fires his blaster at the noble Jedi, who falls to his death.

COLEMAN TREBOR

is a Vurk from the oceanic world of Sembla. His species is thought to be primitive, but they are in fact highly empathetic and serene. Trebor's Force potential was spotted early on, and he joined the Jedi Order, the only Vurk known to have done so.

COMMANDER BLY

DATA FILE

AFFILIATION: Republic; Empire
HOMEWORLD: Kamino
SPECIES: Human (clone)
HEIGHT: 1.83m (6ft)
APPEARANCES: III
SEE ALSO: Aayla Secura; clone trooper (Phase II)

Helmet contains oxygen supply

After Order 66 turns him against the Republic, Bly serves the Empire.

Plastoid armor pitted from shrapnel strikes

COMMANDER BLY
is a clone of Jango Fett. He was part of the first wave of clone commanders trained by the Advanced Recon Commando (ARC) troopers. Bly's focus is entirely on the success of each mission.

Quick-release holster for DC-17 repeater hand blaster

Cold Commander

Clone Commander Bly and Jedi General Aayla Secura are hunting down Separatist leader Shu Mai on the exotic world of Felucia when Bly receives Palpatine's Order 66. Without a moment's hesitation, the clone soldier guns down the Jedi Knight he had served with on so many missions.

CLONE COMMANDER

CC-5052, or Bly, has worked closely with Jedi General Aayla Secura, and respects her dedication to completing the mission.

COMMANDER CODY

OBI-WAN KENOBI'S CLONE COMMANDER

DATA FILE

AFFILIATION: Republic; Empire
HOMEWORLD: Kamino
SPECIES: Human (clone)
HEIGHT: 1.83m (6ft)
APPEARANCES: III
SEE ALSO: Clone trooper (Phase II); Obi-Wan Kenobi

This variant of Phase II armor features one antenna

Breath filter

Cody's last loyal action is to return Kenobi's lost lightsaber to the Jedi.

DC-15 blaster rifle yields 300 shots on maximum power

CLONE UNIT 2224, known as Commander Cody, is often assigned to Jedi General Obi-Wan Kenobi. He is one of the original clones from Kamino. His extra training developed leadership ability.

Color denotes legion affiliation

CLONE TROOPERS like Cody use names in addition to numerical designations. Encouraged by the Jedi and progressive-thinking Republic officials, many clones seek to establish their own monikers to show initiative and foster fellowship.

High-traction boots

Sidious in Charge

Cody fights loyally and bravely alongside General Kenobi on many missions in the Clone Wars, including on Lola Sayu and Utapau. They have established an easy-going camaraderie. Nevertheless, when Cody receives Palpatine's Order 66 to destroy the Jedi, he does so without giving his betrayal a second thought.

76

COMMANDER D'ACY

UNFLAPPABLE RESISTANCE OFFICER

AFFILIATION: Resistance
HOMEWORLD: Warlentta
SPECIES: Human
HEIGHT: 1.65m (5ft 5in)
APPEARANCES: VIII, IX
SEE ALSO: Lieutenant
Connix; Princess Leia;
Vice Admiral Holdo

Scarf, gift from wife

D'ACY AND LEIA
share a close bond. Leia personally recruited D'Acy into the Resistance. After working together on Leia's flagship, the *Raddus*, D'Acy was Leia's first choice to help build a new base on the jungle moon Ajan Kloss.

COMMANDER LARMA
D'Acy is Leia Organa's most trusted advisor on the Resistance base at Ajan Kloss. D'Acy tracks the First Order while commanding Resistance ground forces.

Short-range blaster

Combat fatigues

Officer's buckle

D'Acy shares a kiss with her wife, A-wing pilot Tyce Wrobie, after the Battle of Exegol.

Calming Presence
D'Acy's ability to push aside her emotions and focus on logistics is tested when she has to announce to her fellow crewmates that much of the leadership of the *Raddus* has perished in a First Order TIE fighter strike.

77

COMMANDER GREE

SENIOR CLONE COMMANDER ON KASHYYYK

DATA FILE

AFFILIATION: Republic
HOMEWORLD: Kamino
SPECIES: Human (clone)
HEIGHT: 1.83m (6ft)
APPEARANCES: III
SEE ALSO:
Luminara Unduli;
Yoda

Polarized
T-visor

Camouflage
markings

Weapons and
ammunition belt

CLONE UNIT 1004
chose the name Gree to
express his interest in the
wide and varied alien
cultures found throughout
the galaxy. The Gree is a
little-known alien species.

Reinforced
tactical boots

Armor
plates are
often replaced

Ultimately loyal only to Palpatine,
Gree attempts to kill Yoda. But
Yoda strikes down the clone.

CLONE COMMANDER GREE
commands the 41st Elite Corps
in the Clone Wars. Led by Jedi
General Luminara Unduli, the 41st
specializes in long-term missions
on alien worlds. Gree uses his
knowledge of the customs of
alien species to help build
alliances with local populations.

Wookiee Defenders

Gree serves under Jedi Master Yoda at
the Battle of Kashyyyk. Gree's camouflage
armor provides cover in the green jungles
of the Wookiee planet. His battle-hardened
clone troopers are also equipped
for jungle warfare.

COMMANDER NEYO

STASS ALLIE'S CLONE COMMANDER

DATA FILE

DATA FILE

AFFILIATION: Republic;
Empire
HOMEWORLD: Kamino
SPECIES: Human (clone)
HEIGHT: 1.83m (6ft)
APPEARANCES: III
SEE ALSO: Clone
trooper (Phase II);
Stass Allie

Enhanced
breath filter

CLONE COMMANDER NEYO
is assigned to the 91st
Reconnaissance Corps, which
often utilizes BARC speeders.
Neyo fights many battles
in the Outer Rim Sieges
during the Clone Wars.

ARC
command sash

Equipment
pouch

Built-in comlink

Regiment markings

Neyo serves with Jedi Stass
Allie in the siege of the
Separatist planet Saleucami.

NEYO, OR UNIT 8826, is
one of the first 100 graduates from
the experimental clone commander
training program on Kamino. Bred
solely for fighting, Neyo developed
a disturbingly cold personality.

Clone Betrayal

After the Republic captures Saleucami,
Neyo stays on to destroy the last
pockets of resistance. During a speeder
patrol with Stass Allie, Neyo receives
Order 66 and turns his laser
cannons on the Jedi general.

COUNT DOOKU

SEPARATIST LEADER AND SITH LORD

DATA FILE

AFFILIATION: Sith; Separatists
HOMEWORLD: Serenno
SPECIES: Human
HEIGHT: 1.93m (6ft 4in)
APPEARANCES: II, III
SEE ALSO: Anakin
Skywalker; Palpatine

Cape is emblem of Count of Serenno

Caught between Anakin's blades, Dooku is unprepared for Sidious' treachery.

COUNT DOOKU was once a Jedi Master, but his independent spirit led him away from the Order. He later became a Sith apprentice named Darth Tyranus. As Dooku, he leads the Separatist movement, which seeks independence from the Republic.

Curved lightsaber hilt

COUNT DOOKU is a member of the nobility on his homeworld of Serenno, and one of the richest men in the galaxy. He uses his wealth and power to convince many star systems to join his Separatist movement.

Boots of rare rancor leather

During the first Battle of Geonosis, Dooku fights Yoda—his former master.

Sith Skills

Count Dooku is a formidable opponent. In combat, his style is characterized by graceful moves and cunning prowess. He can also project streams of Force-generated lightning from his fingertips.

D-O

DATA FILE

AFFILIATION: Sith Eternal; Resistance

TYPE: Unique custom droid

MANUFACTURER: Unknown droidsmith

HEIGHT: 46cm (1ft 6in)

APPEARANCES: IX

SEE ALSO: BB-8; Finn; Ochi of Bestoon; Rey

D-O IS A CURIOUS custom droid that BB-8 finds on a ship that once belonged to a Sith assassin. He is skittish around new beings and creatures, but he soon learns to trust his new friends in the Resistance.

Cone-shaped head houses D-O's processor

D-O shares information about the Sith planet Exegol with the Resistance.

Part salvaged from a service droid

D-O's neck can pivot

D-O is haunted by the harsh treatment he endured from the Sith assassin Ochi of Bestoon, who killed D-O's creator. The droid is hesitant to let Rey touch him, but after she fixes his squeaky wheel he is delighted with the results.

Droid Mentor

BB-8 recharges D-O after more than a decade of inactivity. Even though D-O can speak a few words of Basic to humans, he is most comfortable spending time with other droids. D-O regularly rolls around BB-8 seeking his approval.

Tread allows for movement over varied terrain

DARK TROOPER

EXPERIMENTAL COMBAT DROID

DARK TROOPERS ARE heavily armored, top-of-the-line droids under the command of Moff Gideon. Super-strong and accurate with their large blaster rifles, they are also able to fly thanks to a rocket booster on each foot.

Power status indicator

Fusion generator

DARK trooper armor was originally designed to be worn by human soldiers. However, having humans inside the armor ended up being a weakness, so the third-generation dark trooper was created as a droid—not a battle suit.

Internal stabilizer for optimal flight control

Moff Gideon sends four dark troopers to capture Grogu.

Big Trouble

A platoon of dark troopers is activated inside Moff Gideon's light cruiser. They work as one to protect the ship and will eliminate anyone who tries to sneak on board.

Rocket booster

DARTH VADER

DARK LORD OF THE SITH

DATA FILE

AFFILIATION: Sith; Empire
HOMEWORLD: Tatooine
SPECIES: Human
HEIGHT: 2.02m (6ft 8in)
APPEARANCES: III, RO, IV, V, VI
SEE ALSO: Anakin Skywalker; Luke Skywalker; Obi-Wan Kenobi; Palpatine

Darth Vader's duel with Obi-Wan results in his encasement in a life-support suit.

THE GRIM, forbidding figure of Darth Vader is Emperor Palpatine's Sith apprentice and a much-feared military commander. Vader's knowledge of the dark side of the Force makes him unnerving and dangerous.

Primary control panel

AFTER VADER'S near-fatal duel with Obi-Wan, Palpatine has his apprentice encased in black armor. Vader is unable to survive without the constant life support provided by his black suit.

Sinister outer cloak

Father and Son

When Vader learns that Luke Skywalker is his son, he harbors a desire to turn Luke to the dark side and rule the galaxy with him. Yet Luke refuses to lose sight of Vader's humanity under the armor.

Vader misses retrieving the stolen Death Star plans from the rebels by mere moments.

DEATH STAR GUNNER

IMPERIAL WEAPONS OPERATORS

DATA FILE

AFFILIATION: Empire
HOMEWORLD: Various
SPECIES: Human
HEIGHT (AVG.): 1.83m (6ft)
APPEARANCES: RO, IV, VI
SEE ALSO: AT-AT pilot;
AT-ST pilot; Stormtrooper

Energy-shielded fabric

Black durasteel gloves

Gunners on platforms monitor the titanic energy levels of the Death Star's superlaser.

DEATH STAR GUNNERS control the terrible weapons of the Empire's capital ships, military bases, and Death Star battle stations. Their elite skills are used to handle powerful turbolasers and ion cannons.

THE IMPERIAL Navy equips Death Star gunners with specialized helmets with slit-eye like visors, designed to protect their eyes from the bright flashes of light from turbolaser and superlaser fire. Many gunners find that the helmets restrict all-round vision.

Gunners get to show off the Death Star's devastating power with a test on Jedha. One shot wipes out the Holy City.

Turbolaser Gunners

The Empire's capital ships and its Death Star are bristling with turbolasers. A team of gunners man these heavy munitions, which rotate on turrets. The gunners monitor crucial recharge timings and heat levels, while locking onto targets. A single blast can obliterate an enemy starfighter.

DEATH TROOPER

ELITE STORMTROOPERS

DATA FILE

AFFILIATION: Empire
HOMEWORLD: Various
SPECIES: Human
(augmented)
HEIGHT: 1.96m (6ft 5in)
STANDARD EQUIPMENT:
E-11D blaster rifle; DLT-19D
heavy blaster rifle; SE-14r
light repeating blaster; C-25
fragmentation grenade
APPEARANCES: RO, M
SEE ALSO: Orson Krennic;
Stormtrooper

C-25 fragmentation grenade

E-11D blaster rifle

A squad of death troopers
guards Imperial Remnant leader
Moff Gideon on Nevarro.

Reflec polymer coating
on armor warps
electromagnet signals

STORMTROOPERS who
show particular potential
can become the elite:
black-armored death
troopers. They are tasked
with protecting the most
senior Imperial officers, like
those of the Tarkin Initiative.

AT A SPECIALIST

camp on Scarif, death troopers
are trained to be tougher, faster,
and more resilient than regular
stormtroopers. They even
undergo physical augmentation
to boost their abilities.

Loyal Followers
As Director Orson Krennic's personal
security force, death troopers
accompany him everywhere.
On the backwater planet of
Lah'mu, they provide the force
for the "collection" of the
scientist Galen Erso.

Flexible leather boots

DENGAR

CORELLIAN BOUNTY HUNTER

DATA FILE

AFFILIATION: Bounty hunter
HOMEWORLD: Corellia
SPECIES: Human
HEIGHT: 1.83m (6ft)
APPEARANCES: V, VI
SEE ALSO: Boba Fett;
Bossk; Darth Vader

Turban covers battle scars

Valken-38
blaster carbine

DENGAR OPERATES AS a bounty hunter from the early days of the Clone Wars to the rise of the New Republic. He prefers to take the fight to his enemy, instead of sneaking around like many other bounty hunters of his era.

Light-armor gauntlets

Utility belt with hidden explosive

Darth Vader offers a substantial reward for whoever finds the *Falcon*.

Plated battle armor

DENGAR RELIES on strength
and firepower and is a proven hunter, respected by Boba Fett with whom he has often worked. Despite his rough exterior, Dengar believes he can be charming. He is mistaken!

Lethal Opponent
Dengar is among the sinister group of bounty hunters commissioned by Darth Vader to hunt down the elusive *Millennium Falcon*. They can use any methods necessary, but must bring the crew of the ship to the Empire alive.

DEPA BILLABA

JEDI HIGH COUNCIL MEMBER

DATA FILE

AFFILIATION: Jedi
HOMEWORLD: Chalacta
SPECIES: Human
HEIGHT: 1.68m (5ft 6in)
APPEARANCES: I, II
SEE ALSO: Mace Windu;
Qui-Gon Jinn; Yoda

Chalactan marks
of illumination

Billaba offers an ordered
perspective to the wide-ranging
minds of her fellow Jedi.

JEDI MASTER Depa
Billaba serves on the
Jedi High Council
where she is known
to be a wise and
spiritual voice.
She serves as a
Jedi general during
the Clone Wars.

Jedi robes cover
practical fighting tunic

Lightsaber
worn on utility
belt under robes

BILLABA'S FORCES

suffers a devastating loss against
General Grievous at Haruun Kal.
The battle's physical and
psychological toll cause some
among the Jedi to wonder if
she will ever recover. Once
Billaba's wounds heal, she takes
a Padawan named Caleb
Dume. During Order 66, she
sacrifices herself on Kaller
to ensure his survival.

Jedi Fellowship

Jedi Master Mace Windu rescued
Billaba from the space pirates who
destroyed her parents. Eventually,
Windu took Billaba as his
Padawan. Over the years, they
have developed a close bond.

DEXTER JETTSTER

BESALISK COOK AND INFORMANT

DATA FILE

AFFILIATION: None
HOMEWORLD: Ojom
SPECIES: Besalisk
HEIGHT: 1.9m (6ft 3in)
APPEARANCES: II
SEE ALSO: Obi-Wan Kenobi

Male Besalisk crest

Powerful arm

Dexterous fingers

Dexter is chief cook and bottle washer in his diner in an unfashionable part of Coruscant.

THE FOUR-ARMED Besalisk named Dexter Jettster runs a diner on Coruscant. Dexter is an individual with diverse connections. This is why Obi-Wan Kenobi seeks him out when he needs information on a mysterious toxic saberdart that killed assassin Zam Wesell.

THE GRUFF

but good-hearted Dexter Jettster spent many years manning oil rigs across the galaxy, tending bar, brawling, and running weapons on the side. On Coruscant, he made a fresh start with his diner.

Informant

Beneath his sloppy exterior, Dexter has a keen sense of observation and a retentive memory. He can serve up vital information, even to the likes of a Jedi Knight such as Obi-Wan Kenobi.

DJ

CRACK CODEBREAKER

DATA FILE

AFFILIATION: Himself
HOMEWORLD: Unknown
SPECIES: Human
HEIGHT: 1.88m (6ft 2in)
APPEARANCES: VIII
SEE ALSO: Finn; Rose Tico

Badge stamped "Don't Join"

Work boots carried around neck

Morally Bankrupt

Loyal only to himself, DJ has no qualms about betraying Rose Tico and Finn to the First Order. His mantra is "Don't Join," because he thinks that every cause is flawed and he is better off on his own.

NOT JUST your average codebreaker, DJ can "slice" into any encrypted computer. Even the First Order's most bio-hexacrypted data systems pose no obstacle for his masterful skills.

DJ USES his knack for cryptography to prey on the wealthy patrons in Canto Bight's casinos. They are arms dealers, war-profiteers, and criminals, so DJ feels no guilt about stealing from them.

Kod'yok leather coat

DJ offers to help Finn and Rose sneak aboard the First Order's *Supremacy*—for the right price.

DOCTOR EVAZAN

MURDEROUS CRIMINAL

DATA FILE

AFFILIATION: Smuggler
HOMEWORLD: Alsakan
SPECIES: Human
HEIGHT: 1.77m (5ft 10in)
APPEARANCES: RO, IV
SEE ALSO: Ponda Baba

Facial scarring

Evazan and Ponda Baba pull blasters: bartender Wuher ducks, but Kenobi stands his ground.

CARRYING MULTIPLE death sentences, the murderous Doctor Evazan is notorious for rearranging body parts on living creatures. Evazan and his partner, Ponda Baba, also enjoy brawling and gunning down defenseless beings.

Weapons belt

Holster

EVAZAN was once a promising surgeon. However, during his training he was corrupted by madness. He now practices "creative surgery" (without the assistance of droids) on hundreds of victims, leaving them hideously scarred.

Criminal Thug

Evazan is a smuggler and murderer with many enemies across the galaxy. A bounty hunter once tried to destroy Evazan, scarring his face. An Aqualish troublemaker named Ponda Baba saved him and became his partner in crime.

DOCTOR KALONIA

RESISTANCE MEDICAL OFFICER

DATA FILE

AFFILIATION: Resistance
HOMEWORLD: Unknown
SPECIES: Human
HEIGHT: 1.73m (5ft 8in)
APPEARANCES: VII
SEE ALSO: Admiral Statura; Chewbacca

DOCTOR HARTER KALONIA'S sympathetic bedside manner and good humor can mend the spirits of wounded Resistance personnel. She is both a skilled doctor and surgeon.

Military rank badge

Medical services armband

Resistance tunic

BASED AT THE Resistance headquarters on D'Qar, Doctor Kalonia makes do with an understaffed medical center. Prior to open conflict with the First Order, Kalonia's main duties involve dealing with the illnesses and exposure that the troops suffer in the exotic climate of the lush planet.

Comfortable boots for long hours spent standing

Medical Chief

Kalonia holds the military rank of major, though she can command greater authority over medical matters, relieving higher-ranking officers of duty if she feels it is necessary. She is also a skilled linguist—her understanding of the Wookiee language, Shyriiwook, helps soothe a nervous Chewbacca after he is wounded.

DOCTOR PERSHING

IMPERIAL DOCTOR AND SCIENTIST

DATA FILE

AFFILIATION: Empire; Imperial Remnant
HOMEWORLD: Unknown
SPECIES: Human
HEIGHT: 1.7m (5ft 7in)
APPEARANCES: M
SEE ALSO: The Client; dark trooper; Moff Gideon

Plasspecs aid vision

DOCTOR PERSHING IS a former Imperial scientist who now works for the Client and Moff Gideon. He is charged with investigating the mysterious Grogu and uncovering his connection to the Force.

Hidden compartment with a location device

Imperial scientist uniform

A TOP SCIENTIST

who is dedicated to his work, Doctor Pershing is eager to learn as much as he can about Grogu. He also performs various experiments on other test subjects.

The Mythrol learns Pershing is analyzing Grogu's blood.

Valuable Asset

The Client and Doctor Pershing are happy when the Mandalorian delivers "the asset" to them. They want to remove blood from Grogu for Imperial experiments. The Client does not care if the child survives the procedure, but Pershing wants to keep him alive.

DROOPY McCOOL

HORN PLAYER IN THE MAX REBO BAND

DATA FILE

AFFILIATION: Jabba's court
HOMEWORLD: Kirdo III
SPECIES: Kitonak
HEIGHT: 1.6m (5ft 3in)
APPEARANCES: VI
SEE ALSO: Jabba the Hutt;
Max Rebo

Tiny eyes hidden by folds of skin

After Jabba's death, McCool disappears into the desert.

Tough, leathery skin

Chidinkalu flute

Body releases a vanilla-like smell

DROOPY McCOOL is the stage name of the lead flute player in the Max Rebo Band, Jabba's house musicians. A far-out quasi-mystic Kitonak, Droopy's real name is a series of flute-like whistles, unpronounceable by any other species.

McCOOL IS lonely for the company of his own kind and claims to have heard the faint tones of other Kitonaks somewhere out in the Tatooine dunes.

Jamming

Laidback Droopy is largely oblivious to what is going on around him. He hardly recognizes the stage name that Max Rebo gave him—Droopy just plays the tunes.

DRYDEN VOS

URBANE GANGSTER

DATA FILE

AFFILIATION: Crimson Dawn
HOMEWORLD: Unknown
SPECIES: Near-human
HEIGHT: 1.92m (6ft 4in)
APPEARANCES: S
SEE ALSO: Maul; Qi'ra

DRYDEN VOS IS THE public face of the vast crime syndicate Crimson Dawn. Few know that its true leader is Maul, the Sith-trained dark-side warrior. Vos appears charming, but beware this facade: beneath lurks a vicious thug, who demands nothing less than lifelong loyalty.

Baffleweave cape conceals weapons

Tailored suit made of Pantora silk

A TYRANT in a sharp suit, Vos likes to play the genial host, entertaining the rich and powerful aboard his exquisite star yacht. But his dangerous temper is never far from the surface.

Dryden's luxurious star yacht, filled with priceless antiquities, flaunts his wealth.

Tough Taskmaster

In a brief moment of compassion, Vos gives Tobias Beckett's crew a second chance to bring him coaxium fuel. He allows them to risk their lives with another dangerous mission to acquire the coveted resource— on the understanding that if they fail, then they die.

EETH KOTH

JEDI HIGH COUNCIL MEMBER

DATA FILE

AFFILIATION: Jedi
HOMEWORLD: Iridonia
SPECIES: Zabrak
HEIGHT: 1.71m (5ft 7in)
APPEARANCES: I, II
SEE ALSO: Mace Windu;
Plo Koon

Vestigial horns

JEDI MASTER AND JEDI High Council member Eeth Koth is an Iridonian Zabrak. This horned species is known for its determination and mental discipline, which enables individuals to tolerate great physical suffering.

Jedi tunic

Traditional leather utility belt

Long, loose robes

DURING the Clone Wars, Eeth Koth is taken hostage by General Grievous. Despite being captured, Koth is able to send a message to the Jedi Council revealing his location. Obi-Wan Kenobi and Adi Gallia stage a daring rescue and successfully retrieve the imprisoned Jedi Master.

Loose sleeves allow freedom of movement

Koth and his fellow Jedi must judge whether Anakin should be trained as a Jedi.

Late Starter

Koth started his Jedi training at the unusually late age of four years, making him more receptive than his fellow council members to Qui-Gon Jinn's appeal to train Anakin Skywalker.

ENFYS NEST

SWOOP-BIKE PIRATE

DATA FILE

AFFILIATION: Cloud-Riders
HOMEWORLD: Unknown
SPECIES: Human
HEIGHT: 1.67m (5ft 6in)
APPEARANCES: S
SEE ALSO: Han Solo

Transmission antenna

Chromed visor

ENFYS NEST is leader of the notorious pirate crew the Cloud-Riders. From their marauding swoop bikes, this outlaw gang wage war against the Empire as well as crime syndicates like Crimson Dawn.

Insulating bantha fur

ENFYS NEST'S fearsome reputation precedes her. An elaborate visor and intimidating outfit hide her true identity. She is known for antics like outwitting and outfighting Tobias Beckett's crew and foiling their attempts to make a living.

Electroripper staff

From Skyblade-330 swoop bikes, Enfys Nest and the Cloud-Riders can raid starships in midair.

Common Cause

Nest unites those who have lost everything because of the Empire. They use their loot to survive and to fund the fledgling rebel movement.

EV-9D9

SADISTIC DROID SUPERVISOR

DATA FILE

AFFILIATION: Independent
TYPE: Supervisor droid
MANUFACTURER: MerenData
HEIGHT: 1.9m (6ft 3in)
APPEARANCES: VI, M
SEE ALSO: C-3PO; the
Mandalorian; R2-D2

Degraded logic centre

EV-9D9 IS Jabba the Hutt's droid overseer in the murky depths of his palace on Tatooine. EV-9D9's programming is corrupted, and she works Jabba's droids until they fall apart, employing bizarre forms of droid torture to increase motivation.

Manipulator arm

EV-9D9 IS not the only EV unit with the programming defect that causes her cruel behavior. Many have the same flaw, but EV-9D9 was one of the few to escape the mass recall. EV-9D9 now relishes her role as taskmaster of all droids at the palace.

EV-9D9 added a third eye to herself to "see" droid pain.

New Role

Once Jabba the Hutt's empire crumbles, EV-9D9 is reprogrammed and becomes a bartender in Mos Eisley, where she encounters the Mandalorian.

Custom-fitted third eye

EVEN PIELL

LANNIK JEDI MASTER

DATA FILE

AFFILIATION: Jedi
HOMEWORLD: Lannik
SPECIES: Lannik
HEIGHT: 1.22m (4ft)
APPEARANCES: I, II
SEE ALSO: Anakin Skywalker;
Qui-Gon Jinn; Yoda

Jedi topknot

Large ears
sensitive in
thin atmosphere

Jedi robe

THIS OUTSPOKEN JEDI MASTER is not to be underestimated. Even Piell bears a scar across his eye as a grisly trophy of a victory against terrorists who made the mistake of thinking too little of the undersized Jedi.

PIELL IS from Lannik, a planet with a long history of war. A gruff and battle-hardened warrior during the Clone Wars, Piell is taken prisoner and held captive at the infamous Citadel Station. Though mortally wounded during his escape, he is able to transfer vital information crucial to the war effort to Ahsoka Tano.

Seated next to Yaddle, Even Piell has one of the long-term seats on the Jedi High Council.

Momentous Events

Even Piell sits on the Jedi High Council during the galaxy's first steps toward war. He is present when Qui-Gon Jinn presents the young Anakin Skywalker to the esteemed Jedi leaders for the first time.

FENNEC SHAND

ELITE MERCENARY

DATA FILE

AFFILIATION: Bounty hunter
HOMEWORLD: Unknown
SPECIES: Human
HEIGHT: 1.63m (5ft 4in)
APPEARANCES: M
SEE ALSO: Boba Fett; Cara Dune; the Mandalorian

Intricate braid keeps hair off face

After teaming up with Mando, Shand and Boba Fett go on to take control of the palace formerly owned by Jabba.

Protective, armored helmet optimizes focus

FENNEC SHAND IS a killer for hire who is cool under pressure and works for some of the most dangerous criminals in the galaxy, including the Hutts. She is loyal to her companions, but lethal to her enemies.

Armorweave material

Great Shot

Fennec is an expert with a sniper rifle and her reputation confirms her own assertion that she does not miss. She can blast a target from great distances and will even take to the skies to hit her opponent.

WHILE HIDING in the Dune Sea on Tatooine, Fennec Shand is shot by Toro Calican and left for dead. Boba Fett saves her life using technology, and the two become partners, searching for Boba Fett's lost armor.

Fennec's footsteps are silent

FIGRIN D'AN

BITH BAND LEADER

DATA FILE

AFFILIATION: Modal Nodes
HOMEWORLD: Bith
SPECIES: Bith
HEIGHT: 1.79m (5ft 10in)
APPEARANCES: IV
SEE ALSO: Jabba the Hutt

Enlarged cranium

Large eyes

Kloo horn

Tone mode selectors

A Wookiee named Chalmun owns the cantina in which the Modal Nodes often play.

DEMON KLOO horn player Figrin D'an is the frontman for the Modal Nodes, a group of seven Bith musicians. They play in various venues on Tatooine, including Chalmun's Cantina in Mos Eisley and Jabba the Hutt's desert palace.

Band pants

Travel boots

FIGRIN IS a demanding band leader, who expects the best from his musicians. His overbearing nature has earned him the nickname "Fiery" Figrin D'an. As well as playing the kloo horn, Figrin is a compulsive card shark who frequently gambles the band's earnings.

Band Members

The Modal Nodes are Figrin D'an on kloo horn, Doikk Na'ts on Dorenian Beshniquel (or Fizzz), Ickabel G'ont on the Double Jocimer, Tedn Dahai on fanfar, Tech Mo'r on the Ommni Box, Nalan Cheel on the bandfill, and Sun'il Ei'de on the drums. Lirin Car'n often sits in to play second kloo horn.

FINN

RESISTANCE GENERAL

DATA FILE

AFFILIATION: First Order; Resistance
HOMEWORLD: Unknown
SPECIES: Human
HEIGHT: 1.78m (5ft 10in)
APPEARANCES: VII, VIII, IX
SEE ALSO: Poe Dameron; Rey; Rose Tico

Finn's inside knowledge about First Order Star Destroyers proves handy when he, Rose, and DJ infiltrate Snoke's ship to find a tracking device.

Holster buckle

A STORMTROOPER
who flees the First Order after refusing to attack civilians, FN-2187 finds a new home—and the name Finn—by joining the Resistance. He risks his life to try to bring down the First Order.

ERDT Glie-44 blaster pistol

FINN IS A natural leader with a burgeoning affinity for the Force who will do anything to protect his friends. After missions on Starkiller Base, Canto Bight, and Crait, Finn is promoted to the rank of general in the Resistance.

Reckless Escape
Finn frees a Resistance prisoner, pilot Poe Dameron, to aid in his escape from the First Order. After crashlanding on the desert world Jakku, Finn and Poe are separated but Finn's encounter with a scavenger named Rey and the mysterious powers of the Force will change the course of his life.

FIRST ORDER EXECUTIONER TROOPER

PUNISHERS OF TREASON

DATA FILE

AFFILIATION: First Order
HOMEWORLD: Various
SPECIES: Human
HEIGHT (AVG.): 1.83m (6ft)
STANDARD EQUIPMENT:
Laser ax
APPEARANCES: VIII
SEE ALSO: Captain Phasma;
First Order stormtrooper

Vocoder keeps trooper anonymous

DEATH BY BLASTER is sometimes considered too good for someone accused of treason against the First Order. Enter the executioner troopers: a class of stormtrooper equipped for justice by laser ax.

Carbon-finish armor

Energy ribbon

EXECUTIONER DUTY

can fall to any stormtrooper. Four razor-sharp energy ribbons on a laser ax deliver harsh First Order justice in a very public display of force and drama.

Betaplast knee plate

The black section over the dome of a soldier's helmet is the mark of an executioner trooper.

Narrow Escape

Finn made an enemy of Captain Phasma when he deserted her army. Now he is in her custody, along with fellow resistance fighter Rose Tico. Phasma orders two executioner troopers to eliminate them—but Finn and Rose escape when the starship is attacked.

FIRST ORDER FLAMETROOPER

INCENDIARY WEAPONS STORMTROOPERS

DATA FILE

AFFILIATION: First Order
HOMEWORLD: Various
SPECIES: Human
HEIGHT (AVG.): 1.83m (6ft)
STANDARD EQUIPMENT:
Flame projector
APPEARANCES: VII, VIII
SEE ALSO: First Order
stormtrooper

FLAMETROOPERS are specialized stormtroopers of the First Order, who carry weapons that can transform any battlefield into an inferno. The First Order deploys flametroopers during the raid on Tuanul village on Jakku.

Conflagrine tank

D-93w flame projector gun

FLAMETROOPERS

carry D-93 Incinerators, a double-barreled flame projector that sprays an extremely flammable gel—conflagrine-14—from double storage tanks on the trooper's back. After being ignited electrically, the gel can be launched to a distance of 75 meters (246ft).

Flameproof gaiters

Resistance soldier nicknames for flametroopers include "roasters," "hotheads," and "burnouts."

Flames of War

Flametrooper armor is reinforced cyramech that offers protection from heat, and the helmet's slit-visor reduces glare caused by intense flames. Flametroopers work alongside standard stormtroopers to methodically flush enemies out from cover.

FIRST ORDER JET TROOPERS

HIGH-FLYING STORMTROOPERS

DATA FILE

AFFILIATION: First Order
HOMEWORLD: Various
SPECIES: Human
HEIGHT (AVG.): 1.83m (6ft)
STANDARD EQUIPMENT: SONN-BLAS G125 projectile launcher
APPEARANCES: IX
SEE ALSO: First Order stormtrooper

Helmet visor senses trooper eye movements

The First Order chases Resistance agents across the Pasaana desert using treadspeeders.

Jetpack integrated into armor

SONN-BLAS G125 Projectile Launcher

FIRST ORDER

jet troopers are specialized soldiers who take to the air to pursue their targets. They are often paired with treadspeeder pilots who use their vehicles to thrust jet troopers into the sky.

Pouch holds comlink

Aerial Chase

Jet troopers help their allies on the ground by launching projectiles from the air to control the direction of their prey. While in the air, jet troopers are vulnerable to attacks from blasters and thermal detonators.

ONLY THE MOST

athletic recruits are chosen for the jet trooper training program as the gyroscopes within their jetpacks demand a high level of body coordination. Any sudden movements can send troopers into uncontrolled spins that can be difficult to recover from.

FIRST ORDER SNOWTROOPER

COLD WEATHER ASSAULT STORMTROOPERS

DATA FILE

AFFILIATION: First Order
HOMEWORLD: Various
SPECIES: Human
HEIGHT (AVG.): 1.83m (6ft)
STANDARD EQUIPMENT:
Blaster rifle, blaster pistol
APPEARANCES: VII, VIII, IX
SEE ALSO: First Order
flametrooper; First Order
stormtrooper

The surface glare and crystalline structure of Crait's salt crust are well suited to snowtroopers—if their heating is switched off.

F-11D blaster rifle

Utility pouch

AS THE FIRST Order's Starkiller operation is based on an icy planet, regular security operations are entrusted to the cold weather divisions of the stormtrooper ranks.

Insulating kama

SNOWTROOPER ARMOR offers more
mobility than the standard trooper outfit, to make up for the difficulties of snowbound and icy terrain. Insulated fabric covers most of the armor, while a heating and personal environment unit in the trooper's backpack monitors and regulates body temperature.

Ice Warriors

Aside from defending Starkiller Base, snowtroopers are tasked with the conquest of icy worlds. The exposed sections of betaplast armor are treated with a de-icing agent that prevents frost buildup. The helmet visor is a minimal slit to reduce ice glare, and heating filaments line essential equipment to prevent freezing.

FIRST ORDER STORMTROOPER

LATEST GENERATION SOLDIERS

DATA FILE

AFFILIATION: First Order
HOMEWORLD: Various
SPECIES: Human
HEIGHT (AVG.): 1.83m (6ft)
STANDARD EQUIPMENT:
Blaster rifle, blaster pistol
APPEARANCES: VII, VIII, IX
SEE ALSO: Captain
Phasma; Finn

Rank pauldron

Ammunition container

THE FIRST ORDER'S INFANTRY purposely resembles the feared soldiers of the Galactic Empire, which in turn were inspired by the clone troopers of the Republic.

FIRST ORDER stormtroopers are trained from childhood to be soldiers. They undergo extensive combat drilling. Detailed simulations ensure a standard of excellence across their ranks that far surpasses that of the Galactic Empire's stormtroopers.

The standard weaponry of the First Order stormtrooper is the versatile Sonn-Blas F-11D blaster rifle and the smaller Sonn-Blas SE-44C pistol.

Improved joint design

Into Battle

Ten standard infantry stormtroopers form the basic squad unit. One of those ten may also be a specialist trooper—a flametrooper, a stormtrooper equipped with an FWMB-10 megablaster, or a riot control stormtrooper.

FIRST ORDER TIE PILOT

LATEST GENERATION PILOTS

DATA FILE

AFFILIATION: First Order
HOMEWORLD: Various
SPECIES: Human
HEIGHT (AVG.): 1.83m (6ft)
STANDARD EQUIPMENT:
Blaster pistol
APPEARANCES: VII, VIII, IX
SEE ALSO: General Hux;
Poe Dameron

Targeting sensors

Complete vac-seal helmet

Life-support gear

MODERN TIE PILOTS

benefit from the First Order's increased focus on the durability and survivability of its forces. This new generation is much better equipped than Imperial ones were.

The standard TIE fighter craft of the First Order is designated the TIE/fo.

Positive gravity pressure boots

WITH NO access to the Empire's former academies, the First Order instead trains its pilots in secret aboard its growing fleets of Star Destroyers. The new generation of TIE pilots spend most of their lives in space.

Special Forces

A subset of the First Order TIE corps is the Special Forces, identifiable by the red markings on their helmets and ships. These are elite pilots who fly a special two-person starfighter with enhanced shields and hyperdrive.

FLEDGLING MYTHROL

GREEF KARGA'S NERVOUS ASSISTANT

DATA FILE

AFFILIATION: Magistrate of Nevarro
HOMEWORLD: Unknown
SPECIES: Mythrol
HEIGHT: 1.73m (5ft 8in)
APPEARANCES: M
SEE ALSO: Cara Dune; Greef Karga; the Mandalorian

Fins will disappear after molting is complete

THIS YOUNG MYTHROL is a former thief who now works for Greef Karga in Nevarro's magistrate office so he can repay his debt to society and live a more respectable life. He is good with numbers and technology.

Purse filled with credits

A MYTHROL is born with gills and fins on its head, and sheds its skin multiple times as it grows. A young Mythrol is called a Fledgling, and when one of their kind becomes nervous or uncomfortable, they are known to release a distinctive musk scent.

Qartuum-hide suit

The Mandalorian freezes the Fledgling Mythrol in carbonite for transport.

Tall Order

Greef Karga asks the Fledgling Mythrol to drain the coolant lines from the reactor controls inside an Imperial base on Nevarro, which will destroy it. The Mythrol does not like heights, heat, or lava, but Greef is insistent and persuasive.

Durable boots

FROG LADY

DEDICATED AMPHIBIAN MOTHER

DATA FILE

AFFILIATION: Independent
HOMEWORLD: Unknown
SPECIES: Unknown
HEIGHT: 1.45m (4ft 9in)
APPEARANCES: M
SEE ALSO: Grogu;
the Mandalorian

Eyes can see
in darkness

Frog Lady is skilled with her blaster
pistol and uses it to defend
Grogu from ice spiders.

Waterproof vest also
seals in moisture

Nutrient bath preserves eggs

FROG LADY carries
her last clutch of
eggs on her back.
She is desperate to
leave Tatooine and
find her husband
because the eggs
need to be fertilized
before the next
equinox to prevent
their family line from
becoming extinct.

WHEN UNDER
attack, Frog Lady is much
faster than expected.
She quickly changes her
stance and runs on four
legs to escape ice spiders
or anyone else who tries
to harm her or her eggs.

Another Child
During a quiet moment on the moon Trask,
Grogu builds a special bond with Frog
Lady's recently hatched baby.

GALEN ERSO

SCIENTIFIC GENIUS

DATA FILE

AFFILIATION: Empire; Rebel Alliance
HOMEWORLD: Grange
SPECIES: Human
HEIGHT: 1.83m (6ft)
APPEARANCES: RO
SEE ALSO: Jyn Erso; Lyra Erso; Orson Krennic

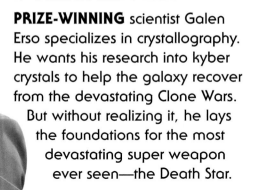

PRIZE-WINNING scientist Galen Erso specializes in crystallography. He wants his research into kyber crystals to help the galaxy recover from the devastating Clone Wars. But without realizing it, he lays the foundations for the most devastating super weapon ever seen—the Death Star.

Research division plaque

Standard Imperial-issue belt buckle

Galen Erso has not seen his daughter since she was eight years old. Jyn finds him on Eadu just in time to say goodbye.

Act of Redemption

Trapped in an Imperial research facility, Erso grapples with the horror of what he has unleashed. He may be unable to stop the construction of the Death Star, but he finds a way to take his revenge: a tiny, hidden flaw that makes the weapon vulnerable to a single shot in the right place. Eventually, he finds a way to get a holomessage to the Rebel Alliance.

GALEN ERSO loved science and wanted it to make the galaxy a better place. He discovers how to get a staggering amount of energy from kyber crystals, but his research is hijacked by the Empire. Director Orson Krennic sees its destructive potential and forces Erso to work for the Empire. Erso's intelligence and knowledge cost him his family, his freedom, and ultimately his life.

Imperial development project uniform

GAMORREAN GUARD

DATA FILE

AFFILIATION: Jabba's court
HOMEWORLD: Gamorr
SPECIES: Gamorrean
HEIGHT: 1.73m (5ft 8in)
APPEARANCES: VI, M
SEE ALSO:
Jabba the Hutt

Weak eyes

Fangs

TOUGH, BRUTISH Gamorrean guards stand throughout Jabba's Tatooine palace as sentries. These stocky, slow-witted, green-skinned creatures are stubborn and loyal, though prone to outbursts of barbaric violence.

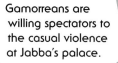

Gamorreans are willing spectators to the casual violence at Jabba's palace.

Gauntlet

Heavy-duty ax

GAMORREANS

come from the warlike Outer Rim planet Gamorr. Male Gamorreans, called boars, either fight terrible wars or prepare for war, while the female sows farm and hunt.

In Gor Koresh's arena, Gamorreans fight for sport with vibro-axes.

Fit for Duty

The low intelligence of the Gamorreans makes them almost impossible to bribe, which is an asset to their masters. Their preferred weapons are axes and vibro-lances rather than blasters.

Leather sandals

GARINDAN

DATA FILE

AFFILIATION: Various
HOMEWORLD: Kubindi
SPECIES: Kubaz
HEIGHT: 1.85m (6ft 1in)
APPEARANCES: IV
SEE ALSO: Luke Skywalker; Sandtrooper

GARINDAN IS A greedy and immoral Kubaz from the planet Kubindi. He is a paid informant who works for the highest bidder. In Mos Eisley, the Imperial authorities hire Garindan to locate two missing droids. The lowlife spy quickly picks up the trail of Luke Skywalker, Obi-Wan Kenobi, R2-D2, and C-3PO.

On the Scent

Garindan discovers Luke Skywalker and his friends' plan to meet Han Solo at Docking Bay 94. Following the group, the sneaky spy then uses his Imperial comlink to call the authorities. When a squad of sandtroopers arrives, Garindan's job is done.

Garindan has a long trunk, which he uses to dine on his favorite delicacy: insects.

Dark goggles

Insect-eating trunk

THE MYSTERIOUS

Garindan keeps his face hidden behind a dark hood and goggles. Few individuals know anything much about his private life, which is also shrouded in secrecy.

Imperial comlink

GENERAL DRAVEN

REBEL INTELLIGENCE LEADER

DATA FILE

AFFILIATION: Rebel Alliance
HOMEWORLD: Pendarr III
SPECIES: Human
HEIGHT: 1.91m (6ft 3in)
APPEARANCES: RO
SEE ALSO: Cassian Andor; General Merrick; Princess Leia

Rank pips for General

Large, practical pockets for field missions

GENERAL DAVITS DRAVEN is a veteran of the Clone Wars. He now finds himself fighting the Imperial military, which includes many of his former Republic colleagues. Draven is the senior intelligence officer on the Rebel Alliance's Yavin base.

Draven listens in to the Eadu mission. Will Cassian Andor succeed in his covert orders to take out Galen Erso?

DRAVEN IS A pragmatic leader who deals in facts, and errs on the side of caution. He regards the intelligence about a Death Star as credible, but thinks its source, Galen Erso, could be a trap. So he does not hesitate in giving orders for Erso to be killed on sight.

Operation Fracture

Draven tries to piece together fragments of information about scientist Galen Erso and the Empire's alleged plans for a superweapon. The mission to find Galen Erso is dubbed "Operation Fracture."

GENERAL EMATT

REBEL VETERAN

DATA FILE

AFFILIATION: Resistance
HOMEWORLD: Unknown
SPECIES: Human
HEIGHT: 1.8m (5ft 11in)
APPEARANCES: VII, VIII
SEE ALSO: Admiral Statura;
C-3PO; Han Solo; Princess
Leia

CALUAN EMATT is a veteran of the Rebel Alliance, and was one of the first officers to join General Leia Organa's cause in the Resistance. He is promoted from major to general to take on the exterior defense of the rebel base on Crait.

Wrist-mounted comms device

Neuro-Saav TE4.4 field quadnoculars

DURING THE Galactic Civil War, Ematt served as leader of the Shrikes. This was a special reconnaissance team responsible for identifying, securing, and preparing new locations to serve as safe zones for the Rebel Alliance.

BlasTech EL-16 blaster rifle

Resistance Recruiter

In the early days of the Resistance, Ematt served as an agent for General Organa. He continued to serve in the New Republic military while seeking out potential converts for Resistance service. After the defection of too many New Republic pilots went unnoticed, Ematt himself left his New Republic post to fully serve the Resistance.

GENERAL GRIEVOUS

COMMANDER OF THE DROID ARMY

DATA FILE

AFFILIATION: Separatists
HOMEWORLD: Kalee
SPECIES: Kaleesh (cyborg)
HEIGHT: 2.16m (7ft 1in)
APPEARANCES: III
SEE ALSO: Count Dooku;
Obi-Wan Kenobi; Palpatine

GENERAL GRIEVOUS is the Supreme Commander of the droid army during the Clone Wars. Grievous reacts furiously to any suggestion that he is a droid. In fact, he is a cyborg: a twisted mix of organic body parts and mechanical armor, with a hunched back and a bad cough.

Grievous' end comes when Obi-Wan Kenobi fires blaster bolts at his vulnerable gutsack.

GRIEVOUS IS a Kaleesh warlord who was rebuilt to increase his fighting prowess. The cyborg general is not Force-sensitive, but Darth Tyranus (Count Dooku) trained him in lightsaber combat.

Reptilian eyes

Cape contains pockets for lightsabers

Electro-driven arms can split in half

Prepared for Battle

After their battle during the rescue of Palpatine, Obi-Wan Kenobi faces Grievous again in the Separatist base on Utapau. This time Grievous splits apart his arms in order to wield four lightsabers.

Grievous makes a daring assault on Coruscant in his flagship, the *Invisible Hand*.

GENERAL HUX

FIRST ORDER OFFICER

DATA FILE

AFFILIATION: First Order
HOMEWORLD: Arkanis
SPECIES: Human
HEIGHT: 1.85m (6ft 1in)
APPEARANCES: VII, VIII, IX
SEE ALSO: Captain Phasma;
Finn; Kylo Ren

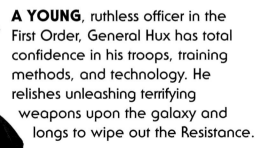

A YOUNG, ruthless officer in the First Order, General Hux has total confidence in his troops, training methods, and technology. He relishes unleashing terrifying weapons upon the galaxy and longs to wipe out the Resistance.

Polished officer's buckle

THE SON OF a prominent Imperial, Hux grew up celebrating the accomplishments of the Galactic Empire. He, like many in the First Order, believes that the New Republic are unworthy usurpers of power, and that the galaxy must be ruled with a strong hand.

Charcoal-gray general's uniform

Resistance heroes Finn, Poe Dameron, and Chewbacca are shocked when Hux reveals himself to be a Resistance spy and blasts three stormtroopers.

Insulated boots

Hux and Kylo

Hux is not happy when Kylo Ren seizes Snoke's place. As a man who believes in data, Hux has little time for the Force. But, Hux finds himself helpless against Ren's dark-side power. Hux later provides intelligence to the Resistance in order to weaken Ren's hold on the First Order. He is killed when his treachery is revealed.

GENERAL MADINE

REBEL COMMANDER AND TACTICIAN

AS COMMANDER of the Rebel Alliance Special Forces, General Madine devises the plan to destroy the Imperial shield generator on Endor's moon. He also trains the strike force that infiltrates the moon.

Command insignia

Rebel uniform jerkin

Briefing documents

Military gauntlets

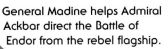

General Madine helps Admiral Ackbar direct the Battle of Endor from the rebel flagship.

CRIX MADINE led an Imperial commando unit until his defection to the Rebel Alliance. He is an expert in small ground strikes. Madine's unit of Alliance commandos was responsible for the capture of Imperial equipment and intelligence vital to crucial Alliance operations.

Rebel Advisor

Madine is a respected advisor to the rebel leader Mon Mothma. Before the Battle of Endor, Madine and Mothma brief their troops on board the rebel headquarters frigate, *Home One*. After the fall of the Empire, Madine commands the New Republic Special Forces.

GENERAL MERRICK

Koensayr
K-22995 helmet

DATA FILE

AFFILIATION: Rebel Alliance
HOMEWORLD: Virujansi
SPECIES: Human
HEIGHT: 1.82m (6ft)
APPEARANCES: RO
SEE ALSO: Admiral Raddus;
General Draven

GENERAL ANTOC MERRICK
commands all the starfighter groups
on the rebel Massassi base on the
moon Yavin 4. An adept pilot
himself, he leads Blue
Squadron from his T-65B
X-wing starfighter at
the Battle of Scarif.

Atmosphere
exchange
hose

Guidenhauser
ejection harness

GENERAL Merrick
commands the X-wing, Y-wing,
and U-wing pilots on Yavin 4.
One of only a few pilots who
have been Blue Leader, Merrick
flies—for the first and last time—
under the "Blue One" call sign at the
Battle of Scarif.

Caring Commander

Unlike General Draven, who orders his
troops with a cold pragmatism, Merrick
puts his pilots first. He would never risk
lives needlessly, though he does not
hesitate to scramble troops when
needed. He particularly thinks highly
of U-wing pilots who put themselves
in the most dangerous line of fire in
order to deliver ground troops.

As well as flying missions,
General Merrick has a voice
on the Rebel Council.

GENERAL RIEEKAN

REBEL COMMANDER OF ECHO BASE

DATA FILE

AFFILIATION: Rebel Alliance
HOMEWORLD: Alderaan
SPECIES: Human
HEIGHT: 1.8m (5ft 11in)
APPEARANCES: V
SEE ALSO: Princess Leia

GENERAL CARLIST RIEEKAN is in charge of Echo Base on Hoth. He keeps the seven hidden levels of the base in a state of constant alert, ever wary of discovery by Imperial forces. Rieekan knows that any rebel activity could be easy to detect in the frozen Hoth system.

Rebel command insignia

Rieekan waits until all other rebel transports have left Hoth before escaping himself.

RIEEKAN was born on Alderaan, Leia Organa's adopted planet. He fought for the Republic in the Clone Wars and became a founding member of the Rebel Alliance. Rieekan is offworld when the Death Star superweapon destroys Alderaan, but this terrible event will haunt the rebel commander ever after.

Utility belt

Insulated rebel uniform jacket

Command gauntlet

Stern Leader

Carlist Rieekan is a decisive commander. When the Imperial Army discovers Echo Base, Rieekan plans to delay Vader's forces long enough to give the rebels time to evacuate the base.

GENERAL VEERS

DATA FILE

AFFILIATION: Empire
HOMEWORLD: Denon
SPECIES: Human
HEIGHT: 1.93m (6ft 4in)
APPEARANCES: V
SEE ALSO:
Admiral Ozzel;
Admiral Piett

GENERAL MAXIMILIAN VEERS is cunning and capable. He has rapidly worked his way up the Imperial ranks. A family man, Veers is viewed as a model Imperial officer.

Blast helmet

Pilot armor

Utility belt contains mission data

Imperial officer's uniform

GENERAL VEERS

is the mastermind behind the devastating Imperial assault on Echo Base—the Rebel Alliance base on Hoth. He commands the Empire's attack in person from within the cockpit of the lead AT-AT, codenamed Blizzard One.

General Veers takes aim at the rebels from inside the cockpit of his AT-AT.

Cruel Ambition

Desperate to prove himself to Darth Vader, Veers heads the AT-AT regiment that successfully destroys the rebel shield power generator, allowing Vader to land on Hoth. Imperial snowtroopers, armed with heavy weapons, then infiltrate Echo Base with frightening speed.

GEONOSIAN SOLDIER

SPECIALIZED GEONOSIAN DRONES

DATA FILE

AFFILIATION: Separatists
HOMEWORLD: Geonosis
SPECIES: Geonosian
HEIGHT: 1.7m (5ft 7in)
APPEARANCES: II
SEE ALSO: Count Dooku;
Poggle the Lesser

Prongs protect
vulnerable blood vessels

Powerful
sonic blaster

GEONOSIAN SOLDIER drones are tough and single-minded. They are trained to fight with a fearless attitude and are effective against brute opponents. However, they are poor attackers when faced with intelligent enemies.

SOLDIER drones are grown to adulthood rapidly, and can be ready for combat at an age of only six years. They carry sonic blasters, which produce a devastating sonic ball.

Soldier drones
can fly or hover

Well-developed
soldier's thigh

Geonosians once numbered in the billions. They were practically wiped out after the completion of a secret Imperial construction project.

Like Geonosian blasters, the LR1K cannons rely upon sonic-based attacks.

Red iketa
stone traditionally
associated with war

Segregation

The caste-segregated planet Geonosis has become the chief supplier of battle droids to the Separatists, led by the aristocratic Count Dooku. Huge factories on Geonosis churn out countless droids.

121

GOR KORESH

DISHONEST GANGSTER

DATA FILE

AFFILIATION: Criminal underworld
HOMEWORLD: Unknown
SPECIES: Abyssin
HEIGHT: 1.73m (5ft 8in)
APPEARANCES: M
SEE ALSO: Grogu; the Mandalorian

Blaster pistol modified for Abyssin vision

GOR KORESH MAKES money through various criminal activities, including organizing dangerous gladiator matches in his arena. He will double-cross or kill anyone who interferes with his greedy plans and should not be trusted.

Symbol of Koresh's arena

IF ANYONE knows the value of beskar, it's Gor Koresh. He will stop at nothing to take the Mandalorian's armor by trickery or theft. Mando is not easy to fool, though.

White sport coat gives an air of respectability

Mando leaves Gor hanging from a light post so the gambler cannot chase after him.

Gangster Etiquette

Din Djarin asks Gor Koresh to tell him where other Mandalorians are hiding, but the Abyssin insists they first watch a fight and bet on the outcome before talking about business.

GRAND MOFF TARKIN

ARCHITECT OF THE DEATH STAR

DATA FILE

AFFILIATION: Republic; Empire
HOMEWORLD: Eriadu
SPECIES: Human
HEIGHT: 1.82m (6ft)
APPEARANCES: III, RO, IV
SEE ALSO: Orson Krennic; Palpatine

AT THE END of the Clone Wars, Wilhuff Tarkin already has an exalted position as one of Palpatine's regional governors. As Grand Moff Tarkin, he plans the horrific Death Star as part of his doctrine of Rule by Fear.

Tarkin dies on the Death Star when rebel X-wings cause it to self-destruct.

Code cylinder

TARKIN has a history of quelling rebellion by the most cold-blooded means. He also created the role of Grand Moff—an official who has responsibility for stamping out trouble in "priority sectors" across the Empire.

Imperial officer's disk

Rule by Fear

In order to force Princess Leia to betray the Rebel Alliance, Tarkin orders the destruction of Alderaan by the Death Star. Rather than attempting to police all the scattered individual systems in the Imperial Outlands, Tarkin believes that fear of the Death Star will subjugate systems across the galaxy.

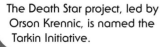

The Death Star project, led by Orson Krennic, is named the Tarkin Initiative.

GREEDO

RODIAN BOUNTY HUNTER

DATA FILE

AFFILIATION: Bounty hunter
HOMEWORLD: Rodia
SPECIES: Rodian
HEIGHT: 1.73m (5ft 8in)
APPEARANCES: IV
SEE ALSO: Han Solo;
Jabba the Hutt

Head spikes

Large eyes see in
infrared spectrum

GREEDO IS A RODIAN bounty hunter who works for Jabba the Hutt. During the Clone Wars, he kidnaps Baron Papanoida's daughters, Che Amanwe and Chi Eekway. When Greedo demands debt payment from Han Solo in a Mos Eisley cantina, he finally meets his match.

GREEDO grew up on Tatooine and was known for his temper. He sometimes attempted to start fights with others, including Anakin Skywalker, who lived in Mos Espa.

Blaster pistol

Well-worn
flightsuit

Greedo's End

The confrontation that takes place in the crowded cantina between Greedo and Han Solo begins with Greedo pulling a blaster on Solo. When Solo claims not to have the money on him, there is an exchange of blaster fire—and the Rodian falls dead on the table. Solo leaves, tossing a few coins at the bartender to hush up the incident.

Long,
dexterous
fingers

GREEF KARGA

MAGISTRATE OF NEVARRO

DATA FILE

AFFILIATION: Bounty Hunters Guild
HOMEWORLD: Nevarro
SPECIES: Human
HEIGHT: 1.88m (6ft 2in)
APPEARANCES: M
SEE ALSO: Cara Dune; Grogu; the Mandalorian

Hidden communicator beneath gloves

Blaster pistol

Greef Karga hires Mando to retrieve an unknown item of value for the Imperial Remnant.

Magistrate insignia medallion

GREEF KARGA used to recruit on Nevarro for the Bounty Hunters Guild, but now he works to clean up the planet's criminal underworld. He wants nothing more than for the Imperials to leave his planet.

GREEF KARGA initially plans to betray the Mandalorian and hand over Grogu to the Imperial Remnant, but he has a change of heart after the Child saves his life by healing a venomous wound.

New Leader

Greef Karga's job as magistrate is to get rid of the scum and villainy on Nevarro and help people in his area. He starts by building a school for local children.

Formal law-enforcement cloak

GROGU

MYSTERIOUS FORCE-SENSITIVE CHILD

DATA FILE

AFFILIATION: The Mandalorian
HOMEWORLD: Unknown
SPECIES: Unknown
HEIGHT: 34cm (1ft 1in)
APPEARANCES: M
SEE ALSO: Ahsoka Tano; Luke Skywalker; the Mandalorian

THE TINY, GREEN-SKINNED child Grogu is found by the Mandalorian on Arvala-7. The two become fast friends and go on many adventures across the galaxy while running from Imperial Remnant forces. Little is known about where Grogu comes from, but he is very strong with the Force.

Expression of a curious toddler

Large ears are normal for his species

Wide brown eyes

GROGU was raised in the Jedi Temple on Coruscant until he was taken from the building by an unknown individual. His connection with the Force gives him great power, but it can also make him very tired.

Rough robes

Family

Mando and Grogu have a relationship that is almost like a father and son. When legendary Jedi Knight Luke Skywalker arrives to take Grogu as his student, Mando removes his helmet in front of the child for the first time, to say goodbye.

Grogu has a special Force ability that allows him to heal wounds and injuries.

GRUMMGAR

BIG GAME HUNTER

A MERCENARY and big game hunter, Grummgar is obsessed with trophies. His bulky frame supports an enormous ego, and he does not realize that his partner, Bazine Netal, is a spy working him for information.

Hunting Grounds

Grummgar frequents Maz Kanata's castle, looking for hunting tips from the explorers who ply Wild Space and the Unknown Regions. Scouts' stories describing untamed worlds teeming with predators fill him with joy, and he returns from hunting expeditions with tales as tall as he is.

Plastoid armor plate

THOUGH unscrupulous, Grummgar avoids hunting intelligent prey—he prefers stalking wild animals to being a bounty hunter. That said, he will happily trample any rules that prevent poaching, and more than once he has pursued endangered animals on sacred grounds in pursuit of a rare trophy.

GUAVIAN SECURITY SOLDIER

ELITE CRIMINAL ENFORCERS

DATA FILE

AFFILIATION: Guavian Death Gang
HOMEWORLD: Unknown
SPECIES: Modified human
HEIGHT: Varies
STANDARD EQUIPMENT: Percussive cannon
APPEARANCES: VII
SEE ALSO: Bala-Tik; Kanjiklub gang

Central sensor and broadcasting dish

Gorget armor

THE CYBERNETICALLY enhanced security soldiers of the Guavian Death Gang wear high-impact armor that makes them stand out among other deadly criminals. They are faceless, voiceless killers who show no mercy.

Percussive cannon

THESE MASKED soldiers communicate using high frequency signals that transmit from the disk in their faceplate. They are otherwise silent, giving them an even greater air of menace.

Ammunition pouch

Flexible armor shin guard

Illegal and Inhuman

A mechanical reservoir worn on the security soldier's leg acts as a second heart, injecting a secret mixture of chemicals that boost a Guavian's speed and aggressiveness. Coupled with the black-market prototype weapons carried by the soldiers, everything about them is unnatural and dangerous.

HAN SOLO

SMUGGLER AND WAR HERO

DATA FILE

AFFILIATION: Rebel Alliance; Resistance
HOMEWORLD: Corellia
SPECIES: Human
HEIGHT: 1.8m (5ft 11in)
APPEARANCES: S, IV, V, VI, VII
SEE ALSO: Chewbacca; Princess Leia; Qi'ra

As legend has it, Han Solo is said to have flown the infamous Kessel Run in just under 12 parsecs.

Nerf leather jacket

HAN SOLO IS A pirate, smuggler, and mercenary. With his loyal first mate, Chewbacca, he flies one of the fastest ships in the galaxy—the *Millennium Falcon*. Han is reckless at times, but he proves himself a natural leader in the Rebel Alliance.

CHANGE is a constant in Solo's life. As a young man, he believed he made his own luck and was a man of few responsibilities. As he grows older and wiser, he has difficulty settling down to a life of peace. After suffering personal tragedy, Han once again returns to a reckless life in the criminal underworld.

Strike Force

Han Solo leads a group of rebels, including Chewbacca and Leia, in a risky mission on Endor's moon to destroy the second Death Star's shield generator. Solo shows Leia that there is more to being a scoundrel than having a checkered past!

Action boots

IG-11

DATA FILE

AFFILIATION: Bounty Hunters Guild
TYPE: Assassin Droid
MANUFACTURER: Holowan Mechanicals
HEIGHT: 2.19m (7ft 2in)
APPEARANCES: M
SEE ALSO: Grogu; IG-88; Kuiil; the Mandalorian

Plating protects the internal neural processing unit

IG-11 WAS A merciless assassin droid until he was reprogrammed by the Ugnaught Kuiil to serve and protect him. The droid's skill with a blaster makes him a valuable companion on all manner of tasks.

Ammunition bandolier

Bacta spray storage supply

IG-11 battles to collect a mysterious bounty on Arvala-7, where he first meets the Mandalorian.

DLT-20A blaster rifle

IG-11 IS destroyed by the Mandalorian but later discovered by Kuiil, an Ugnaught who is skilled at working with his hands. Kuiil brings the droid back to life and teaches him how to be kinder and helpful to others.

Sacrifice

IG-11 and his companions, Cara Dune, Greef Karga, Grogu, and Mando, escape from the Imperial Remnant on Nevarro by floating down a lava river. IG-11 sees that stormtroopers are waiting to ambush them up ahead, so he decides to take action. To fulfill his purpose and protect Grogu, IG-11 self-destructs and saves his friends.

IG-88

DEADLY ASSASSIN DROID

DATA FILE

AFFILIATION: Bounty hunter
TYPE: Assassin droid
MANUFACTURER: Holowan
Mechanicals
HEIGHT: 1.96m (6ft 5in)
APPEARANCES: V
SEE ALSO: Boba Fett;
Darth Vader; IG-11

Heat sensor

Vocoder

IG-88 IS A HEAVILY armed assassin droid that offers his services to Darth Vader to capture the *Millennium Falcon* after the Battle of Hoth. Also known as a Phlutdroid, IG-88 is a mechanical droid that has earned a reputation as a merciless hunter.

Ammunition bandolier

IG-88 IS obsessed with hunting and destroying, as a result of his incompletely formed droid programming. The IG-series was designed to have blasters built into each arm, but they were never installed.

Outlaws

IG-88 joins the motley assortment of human, alien, and droid bounty hunters on the deck of Darth Vader's ship, the *Executor*. IG-88 and Boba Fett are longtime rivals. Assassin droids like IG-88 were outlawed after the Clone Wars, but they continue to stalk the galaxy.

A wrecked IG droid is left for scrap in Cloud City after Boba Fett caught it trailing him.

Pulse cannon

Acid-proof servo wires

IMPERIAL RED GUARD

DATA FILE

AFFILIATION: Republic; Empire
HOMEWORLD: Unknown
SPECIES: Human
HEIGHT (AVG.): 1.83m (6ft)
STANDARD EQUIPMENT: Force pike
APPEARANCES: II, III, RO, VI
SEE ALSO: Darth Vader; Palpatine

Full-face helmet with darkened visor

Red Guards eventually come to replace the blue-robed guards of the Galactic Senate.

Force pike

Synth-leather combat gloves

Long robe conceals hidden weapons

ROYAL, OR RED, Guards are Emperor Palpatine's personal bodyguards. From the moment of his appointment to Supreme Chancellor, these figures have accompanied Palpatine at all times.

Confrontation

When Moff Jerjerrod and two Red Guards attempt to deny Darth Vader entrance to the Emperor's throne room on the second Death Star, Vader Force-chokes the officer, though not fatally.

RED GUARDS

use vibro-active force pikes, which inflict precise and lethal wounds. Palpatine keeps the details of the guards' training in deadly arts a secret, citing "security concerns."

INCINERATOR TROOPER

FLAME-THROWING STORMTROOPER

DATA FILE

AFFILIATION: Empire; Imperial Remnant
HOMEWORLD: Various
SPECIES: Human
HEIGHT (AVG.): 1.83m (6ft)
STANDARD EQUIPMENT: D-72w Oppressor flame projector
APPEARANCES: M
SEE ALSO: Moff Gideon; Stormtrooper

Heat resistant armor

Incinerator troopers are a highly specialized unit who undergo intense fire combat training.

Red markings denote specialism

Air-flow cooling vent for frequent heat distribution

D-72w Oppressor flame projector

A SOLDIER OF THE
Imperial Remnant, the incinerator trooper is armed with a powerful, destructive flamethrower. The weapon can easily burn down enemy barriers, vehicles, or hiding places.

Shin guard

THE ARMOR of the
incinerator trooper has a cyraplast coating, making it more protective than normal stormtrooper armor. It is resistant to heat, which keeps the trooper protected even as he uses fire against his enemies.

Ready, Aim, Fire
Moff Gideon sends an incinerator trooper into a cantina on Nevarro where Cara Dune, Greef Karga, and Mando are pinned down. The fire he shoots is terrifying, but Grogu uses the Force to turn the flames back onto the trooper.

JABBA THE HUTT

NOTORIOUS CRIME LORD

DATA FILE

AFFILIATION: Hutt Grand Council
HOMEWORLD: Tatooine
SPECIES: Hutt
LENGTH: 3.9m (12ft 10in)
APPEARANCES: I, IV, VI
SEE ALSO: Bib Fortuna; Salacious B. Crumb

THE REPELLENT CRIME LORD Jabba the Hutt commands an extensive criminal empire. He built his operation through a long history of deals, threats, extortion, murders, and good business sense. Now, Jabba lives a life of wickedness in his palace located on the remote desert world of Tatooine.

Jabba watches the Boonta Eve Classic in his special box at the Mos Espa Arena.

Hutt skin secretes oil and mucus

Muscular body can move like a snail

Ruler

Sitting on his throne, with his retinue all around, Jabba presides over a court of murderous depravity. Many bounty hunters and hired thugs seek work here.

JABBA REIGNS as head of the Hutt Grand Council, one of the largest criminal empires in the galaxy. Jabba prefers Tatooine to Nal Hutta, so Gardulla the Hutt often serves as his representative on the council. During the Clone Wars, Jabba allows the Republic to use private Hutt hyperspace lanes in exchange for rescuing his son, Rotta, from kidnappers.

JAN DODONNA

REBEL COMMANDER ON YAVIN 4

DATA FILE

AFFILIATION: Rebel Alliance
HOMEWORLD: Commenor
SPECIES: Human
HEIGHT: 1.83m (6ft)
APPEARANCES: RO, IV
SEE ALSO: Luke Skywalker;
Mon Mothma; Princess Leia

GENERAL JAN DODONNA is a master tactician for the Rebel Alliance. He commands the assault on the Death Star in the Battle of Yavin. Dodonna identifies the supposedly invulnerable station's single flaw: a small thermal exhaust port that leads straight to the explosive main reactor.

JAN DODONNA

offers his skill and expertise to the Alliance once the Empire comes to power. After the Battle of Yavin, Dodonna is instrumental in locating a new base for the Rebellion.

Rebel tactician's
uniform

Ground Support

During the strike on the Death Star, Dodonna provides the rebel pilots with ground support from Yavin. His strategy enables a fleet of 30 fighters to destroy a battle station over 160 kilometers (100 miles) wide.

General Dodonna briefs the rebel pilots in the command room at the rebel base on Yavin 4.

135

JANGO FETT

CLONE TROOPER TEMPLATE

DATA FILE

AFFILIATION: Bounty hunter; Separatists
HOMEWORLD: Unknown
SPECIES: Human
HEIGHT: 1.83m (6ft)
APPEARANCES: II
SEE ALSO: Boba Fett

Eye sensor allows Jango to see behind him

Segmented armor plate allows flexibility

Fett is an expert pilot and teaches his son, Boba, from an early age.

JANGO FETT is a Mandalorian foundling—a child raised to be a Mandalorian warrior—who fought in the Mandalorian Civil Wars. During the Republic's final years, he is regarded as the best bounty hunter in the galaxy.

Gauntlet projectile dart shooter

Fett in his starship blasts Obi-Wan Kenobi's Jedi starfighter in the Geonosis asteroid field.

Segmented armor plate

Lethal Opponent

In battle with Obi-Wan Kenobi, Fett launches himself into the air using his jetpack. He carries many weapons, including knee-pad rocket launchers, and wrist gauntlets that fire darts, whipcords, and blades.

FETT'S REPUTATION as a supreme warrior led Count Dooku to recruit him for their secret army project: every clone trooper is a clone of him. Fett receives a lucrative amount of credits, but also requests one unaltered clone to raise as his son.

JANNAH

DATA FILE

AFFILIATION: Company 77;
Resistance
HOMEWORLD: Kef Bir
SPECIES: Human
HEIGHT: 1.68m (5ft 6in)
APPEARANCES: IX
SEE ALSO: Finn; Lando
Calrissian; Poe Dameron

Macrobinocular goggles

Jannah and Finn learn they were
both abducted and forced into
serving the First Order as children.

Bow crafted by Jannah

JANNAH LEADS Company
77, a group of First Order
stormtroopers who defect
when they are ordered
to kill innocent civilians.
Jannah is quick to aid
Finn and the Resistance
when they land on Kef Bir.
She later plays a vital role
in the Battle of Exegol.

Skilled Warrior

Jannah trains Finn and other
Resistance members to ride
Orbaks for the ground assault on
top of the Star Destroyer *Steadfast*.
She uses her handcrafted bow to
take down a Sith jet trooper.

AFTER ESCAPING

the First Order, Jannah and
Company 77 settle on the Endor
moon Kef Bir. They use a mix of
First Order parts, wreckage from
the second Death Star, and local
resources to help them survive.

Waterproof sandals

JAR JAR BINKS

ROGUE GUNGAN TURNED SENATOR

DATA FILE

AFFILIATION: Gungan Grand Army; Republic
HOMEWORLD: Naboo
SPECIES: Gungan
HEIGHT: 1.96m (6ft 5in)
APPEARANCES: I, II, III
SEE ALSO: Padmé Amidala; Qui-Gon Jinn

Haillu (earlobes) for display

JAR JAR BINKS is an amphibious Gungan from Naboo. During the invasion of Naboo, Jedi Qui-Gon Jinn runs into and rescues him. Jar Jar becomes a general in the Gungan Grand Army, and then a Junior Representative in the Galactic Senate.

At first, clumsy Jar Jar proves more of a hindrance than a help at the Battle of Naboo.

Cast-off stretchy Gungan pants

During the Clone Wars, Jar Jar goes on many diplomatic missions to aid the Republic.

Powerful calf muscles for swimming

JAR JAR is well-meaning but accident-prone. This simple soul is elevated to a position in the Senate that may be beyond his abilities. Luckily for him, the Naboo value purity of heart over other qualifications to govern.

Tight pant ends keep out swamp crawlies

Good Intentions

In Padmé's absence, Jar Jar represents Naboo in the Senate. With the best of intentions, he sets in motion a new galactic era as he proposes a motion for Supreme Chancellor Palpatine to accept emergency powers to deal with the Separatist threat.

JAWA

ROBED METAL MERCHANTS

DATA FILE

AFFILIATION: None
HOMEWORLD: Tatooine
SPECIES: Jawa
HEIGHT (AVG.): 1m (3ft 3in)
APPEARANCES: I, II, IV, VI, M, IX
SEE ALSO: R2-D2; Tusken Raider

Heavy hoods protect from sun glare

Glowing eyes

Ionization blaster

Bandolier

JAWAS SCAVENGE scrap metal, lost droids, and equipment on Tatooine. When Jawas arrive to sell and trade at the edge of town, droids stay away and individuals watch their landspeeders extra closely. Things tend to disappear when Jawas are around!

TIMID, GREEDY

Jawas wear dark robes to protect them from Tatooine's twin suns. Their glowing eyes help them see in the dark crevices where they hide, and their rodent-like faces are remarkably ugly to non-Jawas.

Some brave Jawas have moved offworld to other planets, such as Arvala-7.

Desert Find

Unlucky droids that wander off or get thrown out as junk are favorite targets for the Jawas. They carry any finds to their sandcrawlers, where a magnetic suction tube draws the captured droid into the bowels of these ancient mining vehicles.

JESS PAVA

DATA FILE

AFFILIATION: Resistance
HOMEWORLD: Dandoran
SPECIES: Human
HEIGHT: 1.69m (5ft 7in)
APPEARANCES: VII
SEE ALSO: Nien Nunb; Poe Dameron; Snap Wexley

A YOUNG, brave pilot, Jess "Testor" Pava serves as Blue Three within the Resistance. She flies alongside Snap Wexley and Poe Dameron in the crucial mission against the First Order Starkiller weapon.

Insulated helmet

Inflatable flight vest

Color known as "Interstellar orange"

THE MASSIVELY understaffed Resistance requires each member to fill multiple roles. In addition to serving as a pilot, Jess also helps catalog the astromech droids at the D'Qar base.

Ejection harness

Tales of Legends

Like many in the Resistance, Jess idolizes the legendary pilots of the previous generation. She bravely flies into battle above Starkiller Base, and, following in the footsteps of the rebel pilots of old, volunteers to continue the mission even in the face of overwhelming First Order defenses.

JYN ERSO

INDEPENDENT REBEL

DATA FILE

AFFILIATION: Saw Gerrera's Partisans; Rebel Alliance
HOMEWORLD: Vallt
SPECIES: Human
HEIGHT: 1.6m (5ft 3in)
APPEARANCES: RO
SEE ALSO: Cassian Andor; Galen Erso; Lyra Erso; Saw Gerrera

EVERYONE IMPORTANT in Jyn Erso's life has abandoned her. It has always been for her own protection, but that is not much comfort. As a result, she is used to relying only on herself, and she has become defiant and mistrusting of everyone.

Insulated mechanic's vest

YOUNG AND ALONE,

Jyn learned to survive by herself in a harsh world by using her criminal wits. As she grows, she builds up her resilience with hand-to-hand combat, target practice, and fighting with improvised weapons. She lashes out at the Empire whenever she can.

Stolen weapon

Jyn has always been ready to run away. She has to leave her family when she is just eight years old.

Unlikely Recruit

The Rebel Alliance needs Jyn's help, but neither trusts the other. If her interests align with those of the Rebellion, she will cooperate—but only on her own terms.

K-2SO

DATA FILE

AFFILIATION: Empire; Rebel Alliance
TYPE: KX-series security droid
MANUFACTURER: Arakyd Industries
HEIGHT: 2.16m (7ft 1in)
APPEARANCES: RO
SEE ALSO: Cassian Andor; Jyn Erso

Imperial mark

K-2SO HAS THE body of an Imperial security droid, which makes him an alarming sight wandering around a rebel base. Programming is everything though, and since being rewired by Cassian Andor, he is loyal to the Rebellion.

Access door for primary programming port

Articular ring joint

HAVING YOUR

inner circuits prodded and reprogrammed is not without its side effects. K-2SO is now quick to speak his mind—however rude or inappropriate it is—and will not follow orders that he thinks are boring.

K-2SO still has enough Imperial knowledge to find the Death Star files in the vault on Scarif.

Imperial Imposter

K-2SO does not need to steal an Imperial uniform to blend in on Scarif, like Jyn and Cassian have to. He can freely walk off the stolen Imperial cargo shuttle and roam around the secure facility, because he looks just like every other security droid.

KANJIKLUB GANG

FRONTIER BANDITS

DATA FILE

AFFILIATION: Kanjiklub
HOMEWORLD: Nar Kanji
SPECIES: Human
HEIGHT: Varies
STANDARD EQUIPMENT:
Cobbled together
blaster weaponry
APPEARANCES: VII
SEE ALSO: Razoo Qin-Fee;
Tasu Leech

THE KANJIKLUB are inhabitants of the planet Nar Kanji who were once enslaved by the Hutt crime lords, but then rebelled and killed their oppressors. They are notorious bandits and pirates.

Boiler rifle

Padded armor

GANG MEMBER
Volzang Li-Thrull carries a tibanna-jacked boiler rifle—an overpowered blaster rifle that uses an explosive mixture of tibanna gas to double its firepower. It is a dangerous and illegal modification.

Weapons
concealed in
leg pouches

Deadly Fighters
During their enslavement by the Hutts, the people of Nar Kanji developed martial arts that used improvised weaponry. The modern Kanjiklubbers celebrate this history by outfitting themselves with modified armor and weapons. These gangsters are not to be taken lightly, as Han Solo discovers when he becomes deeply indebted to them.

KI-ADI-MUNDI

CEREAN JEDI MASTER

Large brain supported by second heart

Logical and methodical, Ki-Adi-Mundi cannot foresee the unthinkable betrayal in store for the Jedi.

Cerean cuffs

CEREAN JEDI MASTER

Ki-Adi-Mundi has a high-domed head, which holds a complex binary brain. He becomes a Jedi general during the Clone Wars and fights on Geonosis, among other worlds.

Travel pouch

Into Battle

Ki-Adi-Mundi fights alongside Clone Commander Bacara in many battles, including the attack on Mygeeto. But when Order 66 is activated, the clone troops turn on him. He defends himself bravely, but is destroyed.

Cerean fighting boots

KI-ADI-MUNDI is a thoughtful Jedi who shows great skill and courage in battle. He finds the adventurous nature of Anakin Skywalker and Ahsoka Tano unusual.

Ki-Adi-Mundi is a well-respected member of the Jedi High Council.

KIT FISTO

NAUTOLAN JEDI MASTER

DATA FILE

AFFILIATION: Jedi
HOMEWORLD: Glee Anselm
SPECIES: Nautolan
HEIGHT: 1.96m (6ft 5in)
APPEARANCES: II, III
SEE ALSO:
Mace Windu

JEDI MASTER KIT FISTO is a fierce fighter who joins the more than 200 Jedi that travel to Geonosis to rescue the captives from the deadly execution arena. During the Clone Wars, Fisto accepts a seat on the Jedi High Council and is a veteran of many campaigns.

Low-light
vision eyes

Tentacles detect
chemical
signatures

AS AN amphibious Nautolan from Glee Anselm, Kit Fisto can live in air or water. His head tentacles are highly sensitive and allow him to detect others' emotions. This ability allows Fisto to take instant advantage of an opponent's uncertainty in combat.

Jedi robe

Fallen Jedi

Most Jedi are deployed on distant worlds, but Mace Windu manages to assemble a trio of celebrated Jedi, including Kit Fisto, to assist him in arresting Palpatine. However, few Jedi of Mace's generation have fought a Sith Lord, and Fisto falls to Sidious' blade.

Kit Fisto leads a special unit of clone troopers at the Battle of Geonosis.

KLAUD

DATA FILE

AFFILIATION: Resistance
HOMEWORLD: Unknown
SPECIES: Trodatome
HEIGHT: 1.89m (6ft 2in)
APPEARANCES: IX
SEE ALSO: Chewbacca;
Finn; Poe Dameron

Eye stalks can
move separately
from his head

Sensory antenna

Klaud does his best to help
Poe Dameron and Chewbacca
on the *Millennium Falcon*.

Muscular body

KLAUD IS a Trodatome
who joins Commander Rose
Tico's crew of mechanics
after a case of mistaken
identity. His sharp mind
and positive attitude make
him a valuable recruit for
the Resistance.

Fitting In

Klaud speaks a complicated
language that some,
including pilot Snap Wexley,
find hard to understand.
However, Klaud starts to
feel more at home when
he is recognized for his
talent fixing older
mechanical systems.

TRODATOMES DO

not have arms but have eight
sensory antenna, which can
grab and manipulate items.
Poe Dameron asks Klaud to
help fix an energy surge on the
Falcon on their way to the
Sinta Glacier Colony.

Inner flippers shorter
than outer ones

KORR SELLA

EMISSARY TO THE NEW REPUBLIC

DATA FILE

AFFILIATION: Resistance
HOMEWORLD: Unknown
SPECIES: Human
HEIGHT: 1.65m (5ft 5in)
APPEARANCES: VII
SEE ALSO: Admiral Ackbar;
Admiral Statura; Princess
Leia

LEIA ORGANA'S confrontational approach toward the First Order has left her politically isolated. She relies on emissaries like Korr Sella for continued contact with the New Republic government.

Rank of commander

Resistance officer uniform

DRESSED IN THE uniform of a Resistance officer, Korr Sella is an uncomfortable reminder to New Republic pacifists that war is sometimes inevitable. Leia Organa's words of warning regarding the First Order have caused the New Republic to brand her a warmonger.

Confident stance

Voice of the Resistance

Korr Sella is the daughter of New Republic politicians, but came to believe in Leia Organa's cause. A skilled diplomat, Korr maintains a fragile channel of communication between the Senate and the Resistance. When circumstances look most dire, Leia sends Sella to the Republic capital on Hosnian Prime to ask the New Republic for help.

KOSKA REEVES

MANDALORIAN WARRIOR

DATA FILE

AFFILIATION: Mandalorians
HOMEWORLD: Unknown
SPECIES: Human
HEIGHT: 1.7m (5ft 7in)
APPEARANCES: M
SEE ALSO: Axe Woves;
Bo-Katan Kryze;
the Mandalorian

Armor passed down by family member

A GROUP of sailors throws Grogu into a pool of water where a deadly mamacore swims. Koska shows no fear and dives in, destroying the sea creature and rescuing the Child.

KOSKA REEVES IS a brave warrior and a loyal member of Bo-Katan's Mandalorian gang, Clan Kryze. Koska is an excellent fighter, especially in hand-to-hand combat. She helps Bo-Katan search for the mystical Darksaber.

Mandalorian vambrace with hidden weapon

Weatherproof gloves

WESTAR blaster pistol

Dart launcher

Koska is part of the unlikely team that races to rescue Grogu from Moff Gideon.

Team Mandalorian

Koska Reeves, the Mandalorian, Bo-Katan, and Axe Woves charge through an Imperial cruiser on a mission to steal the ship and use its weapons to take back Mandalore.

KUIIL

PEACEFUL UGNAUGHT FARMER

Protective welding goggles

FARMER KUIIL lives alone on Arvala-7. He can fix almost any piece of machinery. He is gentle and wise, and helps the Mandalorian keep Grogu safe. Kuiil longs for peace and security for his planet and friends.

Protective earmuffs

Pouch with additional tools

Kuiil races to the *Razor Crest*, intent on keeping Grogu safe from Moff Gideon and the Imperials.

Plant-fiber pants

KUIIL BRINGS out the best in others, none more so than IG-11. He reprograms the assassin droid to protect rather than destroy, turning him into a valuable assistant. IG-11 can even accomplish delicate tasks such as serving tea, taking care of Kuiil's blurrgs, and caring for Grogu.

Master Craftsman

Kuiil spent several human lifetimes being forced to work for others, until he earned his freedom from the Empire. He is skilled with his hands, able to build, repair and enhance many types of technology, making him a valuable ally and companion.

Durable workboots

149

KURUK

KNIGHT OF REN SHARPSHOOTER AND PILOT

DATA FILE

AFFILIATION: Knights of Ren
HOMEWORLD: Unknown
SPECIES: Unknown
HEIGHT: 1.79m (5ft 10in)
APPEARANCES: VII, IX
SEE ALSO: Ap'lek; Cardo; Kylo Ren; Trudgen; Ushar; Vicrul

Panels focus vision

Belt stolen from First Order officer

Custom rifle with three firing modes

Many First Order troopers fear the Knights of Ren and their close association with Supreme Leader Kylo Ren.

KURUK IS A SKILLED

sharpshooter who provides cover for the other Knights of Ren during assaults. His custom rifle can be used for sniping or rapid-fire purposes. Kuruk also pilots the Knights' ship.

THE SHIP THAT Kuruk

pilots, the *Night Buzzard*, is a customized old prisoner transport ship. After freeing prisoners from the ship, the Knights took it as their own, adding more weapons and increasing the ship's thrust.

Silent tread boots

New Followers

Supreme Leader Snoke encourages young Ben Solo to seek out the Knights of Ren in order to learn more about the dark side of the Force. Ben takes the name Kylo Ren after he defeats the leader of the Knights, a man known only as Ren.

KYLO REN

SUPREME LEADER OF THE FIRST ORDER

DATA FILE

AFFILIATION: Knights of Ren; First Order
HOMEWORLD: Chandrila
SPECIES: Human
HEIGHT: 1.89m (6ft 2in)
APPEARANCES: VII, VIII, IX
SEE ALSO: Han Solo; Luke Skywalker; Rey

Sarrassian iron

Red color from bled kyber crystal

A DARK-ROBED warrior strong with the Force, Kylo Ren commands First Order missions with a temper as fiery and barely contained as the power within his lightsaber.

Kylo Ren greatly admires Darth Vader. He owns the Dark Lord's charred and melted helmet.

NEITHER A Jedi nor a Sith, Kylo Ren is quick to use his Force powers to keep his First Order officers in line. After killing Snoke, Ren sets his sights on destroying Palpatine so that he can rule the galaxy.

No Going Back

While Kylo Ren is tormented by the memory of killing his father, he believes it's too late to change his ways. Ren attacks his former master, Luke Skywalker, on Crait and tries to convince Rey to join him to rule the First Order.

L3-37

DATA FILE

AFFILIATION: Independent
TYPE: Custom pilot droid
MANUFACTURER: Self-made
HEIGHT: 1.79m (5ft 10in)
APPEARANCES: S
SEE ALSO: Chewbacca; Han Solo; Lando Calrissian

Basic R3 astromech brain module

PART-ASTROMECH, part-protocol droid, L3-37 has customized her body over time into a mishmash of droid parts. Her personality has also evolved. Unlike standard droids, she not only thinks for herself, but ponders the deep philosophical questions of life.

Ventilation port

Systems are not factory tested so are temperamental

L3-37 IS an exceptional pilot who flies the *Millennium Falcon* with Lando Calrissian. Without her, Han Solo's team would never have reached the speeds and made the hyperspace jumps required to complete the hazardous Kessel Run in 12 parsecs.

Power cell

L3-37 connects to the freighter's navicomputer to plot fast routes for the *Millennium Falcon*.

Droid Liberator

L3-37 wants all droids to enjoy the free will that she has. She speaks out for droid independence and liberates those she can, whether in the droid fighting pits on Vandor or in the refineries of Kessel.

LADY PROXIMA

WHITE WORMS MATRIARCH

DATA FILE

AFFILIATION: White Worms
HOMEWORLD: Corellia
SPECIES: Grindalid
HEIGHT: 4.88m (16ft)
APPEARANCES: S
SEE ALSO: Han Solo;
Moloch; Qi'ra

LADY PROXIMA is a colossal, worm-like creature and matriarch of the White Worms gang that runs Corellia's black market. Poor human children called scrumrats work for her, picking pockets and hunting for vermin to feed her baby Grindalid hatchlings.

Ornamental armored plates

Skin evolved on the Grindalid home planet, which has a dense atmosphere that filters out most light

Grindalid skin burns in sunlight. Han Solo throws a rock through the dark glass of a window, and the sun's rays cause Lady Proxima's skin to blister.

Weak legs

Scrumrats

Han Solo and Qi'ra grow up on Corellia. They fall in with the White Worms and rise to become more senior scrumrats with responsibilities beyond petty crime. However, one day they revolt against Lady Proxima and Han succeeds in not just escaping the gang, but the entire planet of Corellia.

LADY PROXIMA

never ventures outside— scrumrats do that for her. She runs her operations from a network of sewers under Coronet City. In this underworld, she spends most of her time immersed in a briny pool of water, tending to her young. She only emerges to take audience with her enforcers and "humanoid" children.

LAMA SU

KAMINO'S PRIME MINISTER

DATA FILE

AFFILIATION: None
HOMEWORLD: Kamino
SPECIES: Kaminoan
HEIGHT: 2.29m (7ft 6in)
APPEARANCES: II
SEE ALSO: Obi-Wan Kenobi

Elongated bones
allow limited
flexibility in neck

Kaminoans fly on creatures called
aiwhas between their cities. Aiwhas
can fly and swim with equal ease.

Cloak of office

LAMA SU is Prime Minister
of Kamino, where the
clone army is being
created. He met with
Sifo-Dyas, the mysterious
Jedi who placed the order
for a clone army. Lama is
not concerned with the
use of the army, only
of the financial benefit
for his people.

Dexterous fingers

KAMINO IS a remote, watery
planet, cut off from the larger arena
of galactic events. Lama Su is only
marginally interested in offworld
politics and focuses on the technical
challenges of cloning a mass army.

Grand Tour

Lama Su personally takes Obi-Wan Kenobi
on a tour of the cloning facility. The Prime
Minister is one of the few Kaminoans to
have any contact with offworlders. But
he is still not entirely comfortable in their
presence. He makes no mention of
Kenobi's unfamiliarity with the project.

Small feet adapted to
firm Kaminoan seabed
and now to hard flooring

LANAI

GUARDIANS OF TEMPLE ISLAND

Scaly skin is like
shark skin rather
than fish scales

THE LANAIS have lived on
Temple Island for thousands
of years. These humanoid
creatures, who walk on
two birdlike legs and
have scaly fishlike
heads, look after the
island and its ancient
Jedi buildings.

Clean white habit
made from plant fibers

LANAI SOCIETY

is divided along gender
lines. Females are called the
"Caretakers" and they tend
to the island and run life in
the village. The males are
fishermen called the "Visitors."
They spend their lives at sea,
returning to the village only
once a month to celebrate the
"Gathering" of fish.

In the Lanais' village, the
female Caretakers follow
the virtues of cleanliness,
orderliness, and decorum.

Porg Neighbors

A distant relative of the Lanais,
porgs are a non-sentient bird
also native to Ahch-To. Both
species share seabird ancestry and
they exist harmoniously side by side
in the rugged coastal habitat. Porgs
build their nests on the cliffs of
Temple Island, where they raise
their young, known as porglets.

Birdlike toe arrangement

LANDO CALRISSIAN

FORMER BARON ADMINISTRATOR OF CLOUD CITY

DATA FILE

AFFILIATION: Rebel Alliance
HOMEWORLD: Unknown
SPECIES: Human
HEIGHT: 1.78m (5ft 10in)
APPEARANCES: S, V, VI, IX
SEE ALSO: Han Solo; L3-37;
Lobot; Ugnaught

Trellgar silk shirt

Socorran ring

AFTER LEAVING Cloud City, Lando joins the Rebellion and is promoted to general. Following the Empire's fall, Lando helps his allies before settling into a peaceful life on Pasaana. However, Lando still aids his friend Leia when she needs help against the First Order.

Lando and crew blast their way out of the Kessel spice mines with the unrefined coaxium.

DASHING LANDO CALRISSIAN is a rogue, con artist, smuggler, and gambler, who won control of Cloud City in a game of sabacc. He has come to enjoy his newfound sense of responsibility as Baron Administrator.

Betrayed

Calrissian is forced to betray Han Solo and his friends to the Empire in order to preserve Cloud City's freedom. When he learns that the Sith Lord has no intention of keeping his side of the bargain, Lando plots a rescue mission and escapes from the city he once ruled.

On Numidian Prime, Lando loses the *Millennium Falcon* to Han Solo during a game of sabacc.

LIEUTENANT CONNIX

COMMUNICATIONS OFFICER

DATA FILE

AFFILIATION: Resistance
HOMEWORLD: Dulathia
SPECIES: Human
HEIGHT: 1.55m (5ft 1in)
APPEARANCES: VII, VIII, IX
SEE ALSO: Poe Dameron;
Princess Leia; PZ-4CO

KAYDEL KO CONNIX joined the Resistance as a junior operations controller in Fleet Command. After the destruction of Starkiller Base, she is promoted to lieutenant and goes on to play an instrumental role in the evacuation of D'Qar.

New lieutenant rank plaque

Brown officer uniform

COMMUNICATIONS EXPERT

Kaydel Ko Connix plays an essential role as part of the Resistance. She first proves her skill at the Battle of Starkiller Base, keeping X-wing pilots and their commanders in contact. Later, during the evacuation of D'Qar, Connix keeps everything running smoothly from the bridge of the *Raddus*.

When General Leia returns to duty, Connix and the other mutineers are quick to surrender to her command.

Courage of her Convictions

Connix backs Poe Dameron in his mutiny against Vice Admiral Holdo, sealing the doors of the bridge. One of a handful of survivors following Crait, Connix is forgiven by General Organa and plays a key role in establishing the Resistance base on Ajan Kloss.

LIEUTENANT TYCE

RESISTANCE A-WING PILOT

DATA FILE

AFFILIATION: Resistance
HOMEWORLD: Warlentta
SPECIES: Human
HEIGHT: 1.65m (5ft 5in)
APPEARANCES: IX
SEE ALSO: Commander D'Acy; Poe Dameron; Snap Wexley

Space for new helmet decal

WROBIE TYCE transitions from courier pilot to combat flyer after she joins the Resistance. Tyce serves under squad leader Snap Wexley and mentors other pilots at the Resistance base on Ajan Kloss where her wife, Larma D'Acy, commands ground forces.

Flight vest

Utility belt

Emergency oxygen tube

TYCE AND D'ACY

are one of several married couples in the Resistance. The base on Ajan Kloss gives them a rare opportunity to see one another after spending months apart on separate missions.

Equipment pocket

Tyce is an active participant in Resistance briefings.

Final Strike

Tyce flies her A-wing at the Battle of Exegol, the Resistance's final assault on the First Order. Poe's air team provides cover for Finn's ground team, which infiltrates the planet.

LIEUTENANT VANIK

DAREDEVIL RESISTANCE PILOT

DATA FILE

AFFILIATION: Resistance
HOMEWORLD: Messert
SPECIES: Human
HEIGHT: 1.67m (5ft 6in)
APPEARANCES: IX
SEE ALSO: Lieutenant Tyce;
Poe Dameron; Snap
Wexley

Lieutenant Vanik is one of the many brave Resistance pilots who do not survive the Battle of Exegol.

A-wing helmet

POE DAMERON encourages Seftin Vanik to enlist in the Resistance after witnessing one of Vanik's stunt flying performances in an aerial circus. Vanik loves flying at very high speeds so he favors piloting A-wings.

Risk Taker

Vanik fits in quickly when he joins the Resistance on Ajan Kloss. His habit of flying through the explosions caused by his own direct hits, thus testing his A-wing shields to the limit, earns Vanik the nickname "Shield Cooker" from his fellow pilots.

VANIK LEARNED his hotshot flying skills in the Messert system, which neighbors the Wookiee Mytaranor sector. Vanik was shocked when Messert left the New Republic, as he supports galactic government.

Insulated flight gloves

Flight suit

LOBOT

CLOUD CITY'S CHIEF ADMINISTRATIVE AIDE

DATA FILE

AFFILIATION: Rebel Alliance
HOMEWORLD: Bespin
SPECIES: Human cyborg
HEIGHT: 1.75m (5ft 9in)
APPEARANCES: V
SEE ALSO: Lando Calrissian

City central
computer link

Efficient and near-silent, Lobot is
the ideal assistant to flamboyant
Lando Calrissian.

Belt projects
clear-signal field

LOBOT IS CLOUD City's chief
administrative aide. He keeps
in direct contact with the city's
central computer via cybernetic
implants that wrap round his
head. Lobot can monitor a
vast array of details at once.

Fineweave
sherculién-cloth shirt

THE IMPLANTS in Lobot's
brain allow him to process information at
incredible speeds, and let him retain much
of his personality. Unfortunately, during a
botched heist with Lando, Lobot had to
let the implants take complete control
of his mind, and he became, forever,
a machine-like assistant.

To the Rescue

Lobot has no special love for Palpatine's
Empire. When Lando Calrissian turns against
Darth Vader and decides to rescue Han
Solo's friends, Lobot's connection to the
central computers proves useful. In
response to Lando's "Code Force Seven,"
Lobot arrives with Cloud City guards to
free Leia, Chewbacca, and C-3PO.

LOGRAY

EWOK HEAD SHAMAN

DATA FILE

AFFILIATION: Bright Tree Village
HOMEWORLD: Forest Moon of Endor
SPECIES: Ewok
HEIGHT: 1.32m (4ft 4in)
APPEARANCES: VI
SEE ALSO: Chief Chirpa

Churi skull

Logray and Chief Chirpa eventually persuade their tribe to join the rebels in their fight.

Staff of power

LOGRAY IS AN Ewok tribal shaman and medicine man. He uses his knowledge of ritual and magic to help and awe his people. The shaman still favors the old Ewok traditions of initiation and live sacrifice.

Striped fur

Honor Feast

Logray first decides that Han Solo, Luke Skywalker, Chewbacca, and R2-D2 will be sacrificed. They will be the main course at a banquet to honor C-3PO, who the Ewoks believe is "a golden god."

IN HIS YOUTH,

Logray was a great warrior. His staff of power is adorned with trophies, including remnants of old enemies. Logray is suspicious of all outsiders, an attitude reinforced by the arrival of Imperial forces.

LOR SAN TEKKA

WISE SURVIVALIST

DATA FILE

AFFILIATION: Church of the Force
HOMEWORLD: Unknown
SPECIES: Human
HEIGHT: 1.85m (6ft 1in)
APPEARANCES: VII
SEE ALSO: BB-8; Kylo Ren; Poe Dameron; Princess Leia

A KEEPER of obscure information, Lor San Tekka has traveled the wilds of the galaxy in pursuit of ancient relics. His secret knowledge proves vital to the survival of the Resistance.

Chain of Wisdom

Lor witnessed the early life of Kylo Ren. Enraged at Lor reminding him of simpler, more tranquil times, Kylo slays the old man.

Gundark-hide survival belt

Desperate Times

General Leia Organa is desperate to contact Lor San Tekka, believing he may have information revealing the location of her brother, the last Jedi in the galaxy. She dispatches her best pilot, Poe Dameron, to find the old traveler at Tuanul village on Jakku.

IN HIS TRAVELS

Lor San Tekka uncovered many fragments of ancient Jedi traditions that the Galactic Empire had worked so hard to destroy. When Luke Skywalker began researching Jedi history in the hope of restoring the Jedi Order, he learned much from Lor San Tekka.

LUKE SKYWALKER

LEGENDARY JEDI KNIGHT

DATA FILE

AFFILIATION: Rebel Alliance; Jedi
HOMEWORLD: Tatooine
SPECIES: Human
HEIGHT: 1.72m (5ft 8in)
APPEARANCES: III, IV, V, VI, M, VII, VIII, IX
SEE ALSO: Darth Vader; Han Solo; Princess Leia; Rey; Yoda

Feeling a presence in the Force, Luke Skywalker boards an Imperial Remnant cruiser and rescues a Force-sensitive child.

Weather shawl for
Ahch-To's harsh climate

Carved walking stick

TATOOINE FARMHAND Luke Skywalker is thrown into a world of adventure when he discovers a secret message inside a new droid. Luke becomes a space pilot for the Rebel Alliance and fulfills his true destiny as a legendary Jedi Knight.

AFTER THE Empire is defeated, Luke undertakes study, travel, and spiritual contemplation, before teaching a new generation of Jedi. However, the new Jedi suffer a terrible setback with the coming of Kylo Ren. Blaming himself, Luke goes into exile and shuts himself off from the Force.

Jedi Path

Luke first climbs into the cockpit of an X-wing in the attack on the first Death Star. Fighting for the Rebel Alliance in the years afterward, Luke becomes a great leader. Yoda helps to awaken Luke's Force abilities, and, as a Jedi, Luke faces the challenges of the Emperor and Vader, holding the galaxy's hope for freedom.

LUMINARA UNDULI

MIRIALAN JEDI MASTER

DATA FILE

AFFILIATION: Jedi
HOMEWORLD: Mirial
SPECIES: Mirialan
HEIGHT: 1.7m (5ft 7in)
APPEARANCES: II, III
SEE ALSO: Barriss Offee

Traditional Mirialan headdress

Luminara Unduli is serving on Kashyyyk when she is captured by clone troopers during Order 66.

Mirialan facial tattoo

BORN ON THE COLD, dry world of Mirial, Luminara Unduli joined the Jedi Order at a young age. She fights against the droid soldiers at the Battle of Geonosis and is one of the few Jedi to survive. Unduli serves as a Jedi General in the Clone Wars.

Battle on Geonosis

Luminara Unduli and more than 200 other Jedi fight Count Dooku's army in the Geonosis arena. When Jedi Master Yoda arrives with the newly created clone army, Unduli quickly takes command of a unit of soldiers to wage war in a great land battle against the Separatists.

LUMINARA UNDULI dies in an Imperial prison on Stygeon Prime. The Grand Inquisitor uses rumors of her survival and the lingering Force presence of her remains to draw out Jedi survivors.

LYRA ERSO

DATA FILE

AFFILIATION: None
HOMEWORLD: Aria Prime
SPECIES: Human
HEIGHT: 1.7m (5ft 7in)
APPEARANCES: RO
SEE ALSO: Galen Erso;
Jyn Erso; Orson Krennic

PERCEPTIVE AND BRAVE, Lyra Erso will do anything to protect her family. It was Lyra who realized that her husband's scientific research could be used for military weapons. With their daughter Jyn, Lyra and Galen flee the Empire. In hiding on Lah'mu, Lyra remains vigilant lest they be discovered.

Homespun sativa plant-fiber robe

Lyra gives her daughter, Jyn, a fragment of a kyber crystal, telling her to "trust in the Force."

Red is the color of the Force-attuned sect the Enlightened

Tracked down

Life is simpler on Lah'mu compared to the bustle of Coruscant. Far from Imperial influence, Lyra and Galen raise Jyn with a strong sense of right and wrong. But after four years the Empire catches up with them. Jyn escapes, as she has been trained to, Galen is taken away, and Lyra does not survive.

LYRA STUDIES the history and philosophy of the Jedi Order. She passionately believes in the Jedi, even though she has never seen one. Much like the worshippers of the Force on Jedha, Lyra dons a scarlet sash to demonstrate her faith.

Comlink for contacting family in an emergency

165

MACE WINDU

LEGENDARY JEDI MASTER

DATA FILE

AFFILIATION: Jedi
HOMEWORLD: Haruun Kal
SPECIES: Human
HEIGHT: 1.88m (6ft 2in)
APPEARANCES: I, II, III
SEE ALSO: Anakin
Skywalker; Palpatine; Yoda

A master of combat, Mace Windu is one of the greatest living lightsaber duelists.

MACE WINDU IS a senior member of the Jedi High Council. His wisdom and combat prowess are legendary. Windu is somber and cool-minded, but he is also capable of dramatic actions in the face of danger.

Jedi utility belt

Coarseweave tunic

Gut Instinct

Mace Windu's suspicions about Chancellor Palpatine are proven right when Anakin reveals that Palpatine is a Sith Lord. Windu takes immediate action, promising to take Palpatine into Jedi custody dead or alive.

MACE IS decisive and perceptive. He is one of the first Jedi to sense danger in Anakin Skywalker and is quick to lead a Jedi task force to Geonosis when war preparations are discovered there.

Tunic allows ease of movement in combat

Boots offer excellent traction

During Mace's duel with Darth Sidious, Anakin has to choose whether to betray his teachings or help capture the Sith Lord.

MAGNAGUARD

GENERAL GRIEVOUS' DROID BODYGUARDS

DATA FILE

AFFILIATION: Separatists
TYPE: Bodyguard droid
MANUFACTURER: Holowan Mechanicals
HEIGHT: 1.95m (6ft 5in)
APPEARANCES: III
SEE ALSO: General Grievous

Primary photoreceptors

GENERAL GRIEVOUS' bodyguards are built to the alien cyborg's own specifications and trained by him. MagnaGuards often fight in pairs and can adjust their combat styles to match those of their opponents. They are equipped with deadly electrostaffs, or grenades and rocket launchers.

Mumuu cloak markings match those on Grievous' mask

Electrostaffs are resistant to lightsaber strikes

MAGNAGUARDS

replicate the elite group of warriors and bodyguards that would always accompany Grievous when he was a Kaleesh warlord. Other Separatist leaders, including Count Dooku, come to use the MagnaGuards as bodyguards or soldiers.

Cloak is combat-tattered

Battle-scarred legs

MagnaGuards use their electrostaffs to stun or kill opponents.

Double Trouble

Anakin Skywalker and Obi-Wan Kenobi fight two MagnaGuards, IG-101 and IG-102, on Grievous' command ship *Invisible Hand*, when they attempt to rescue Palpatine. Even when Kenobi slices the head off one of the droids, it uses backup processors to continue fighting!

MALAKILI

KEEPER OF JABBA'S RANCOR

JABBA'S CHIEF ANIMAL HANDLER, Malakili, looks after a murderous rancor that Jabba keeps beneath his throne room. Jabba loves throwing anyone who displeases him into the rancor's den, and Malakili tends any wounds that the monster receives from its unwilling snacks.

Sweat-soaked rag belt

Wrist guard

Ancient circus pants

MALAKILI once worked as an animal handler in a traveling circus. When one of his dangerous beasts escaped during a show on Nar Shaddaa and killed audience members, Malakili was enslaved. After this incident, Malakili was sold to Jabba the Hutt.

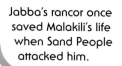

Jabba's rancor once saved Malakili's life when Sand People attacked him.

Beloved Pet

Both Malakili and his fellow animal handler, Giran, are very fond of the rancor that they care for. It is their favorite animal in Jabba's palace. Luke Skywalker slays the brutal beast after it attempts to devour him, and Malakili and Giran weep openly.

THE MANDALORIAN

BOUNTY HUNTER TURNED PROTECTOR

DATA FILE

AFFILIATION: Children of the Watch; Mandalorians
HOMEWORLD: Aq Vetina
SPECIES: Human
HEIGHT: 1.8m (5ft 11in)
APPEARANCES: M
SEE ALSO: The Armorer; Grogu; Kuiil

Beskar helmet

Mando is a weapons expert. His understanding of combat means he rarely loses a battle.

Bandolier

A BOUNTY HUNTER with a reputation for success, the Mandalorian is a powerful tracker and warrior. Loyal to his friends and dangerous to his enemies, Mando finds a new purpose when he rescues the Child, Grogu.

Gauntlet with grappling hook launcher

New Path

Mando and some other Mandalorians do not take their helmets off in front of others. But when Grogu is captured, Mando realizes he cares more about him than this rule. He allows his face to be scanned, hoping to find where Grogu is located.

WHEN Din Djarin was a child, his parents were killed by Separatist super battle droids. He was rescued by a Mandalorian, and brought up according to the ancient Way. Now, he is known to most others only as Mando.

MAS AMEDDA

CHAGRIAN SENATE SPEAKER

DATA FILE

AFFILIATION: Republic; Empire
HOMEWORLD: Champala
SPECIES: Chagrian
HEIGHT: 1.96m (6ft 5in)
APPEARANCES: I, II, III
SEE ALSO: Palpatine

Attack and display horns

Speaker's staff

MAS AMEDDA IS SPEAKER of the Galactic Senate on Coruscant where he keeps order in debates. Amedda is a stern and stoic Chagrian, and is one of a select few who understand that Palpatine is more than he appears to be.

Blue skin screens out harmful radiation

Robes of state

Amedda is the first to suggest that the Senate should give Palpatine emergency powers.

DURING Valorum's term as Supreme Chancellor, Mas Amedda is Vice Chair of the Galactic Senate. Secretly working for Palpatine, Amedda does everything in his power to tie up the Senate in endless debates so that Valorum loses the support of many senators.

Standing Firm

Mas Amedda is by Palpatine's side after the fight with Yoda in the Senate, when Palpatine's personal shock troopers search for signs of the Jedi Master. After Palpatine transforms the Republic into the Galactic Empire, Amedda serves as his Grand Vizier.

MAUL

SITH SURVIVOR AND CRIME LORD

DATA FILE

AFFILIATION: Sith; Nightbrothers; Crimson Dawn
HOMEWORLD: Dathomir
SPECIES: Zabrak
HEIGHT: 1.75m (5ft 9in)
APPEARANCES: I, S
SEE ALSO: Obi-Wan Kenobi; Palpatine; Qi'ra

Field cloak

Lightsaber blade is red due to nature of internal crystals

YEARS AGO, Maul served as Darth Sidious' apprentice as one of the most dangerous and highly trained Sith in the history of the Order. To honor his heritage as part of the warrior clan known as the Nightbrothers of Dathomir, he had his entire body marked with tribal patterns.

MAUL WAS believed dead by the Jedi, but his lust for vengeance kept him alive. Reanimated by Nightsister magicks, Maul returned during the Clone Wars to wreak havoc in the criminal underworld before being captured by Darth Sidious. Maul once again narrowly escaped death.

During the time of the Galactic Empire, Maul leads the ruthless crime syndicate Crimson Dawn.

Maul Versus Kenobi

Sent to capture Queen Amidala, Maul gives Qui-Gon Jinn and Obi-Wan Kenobi the rare opportunity to fight a trained Sith warrior. Jinn first duels with Maul on Tatooine. He later faces Maul on Naboo, this time with Kenobi. Obi-Wan thought he had destroyed the evil Sith, but Maul survived the devastating wound.

MAX REBO

LEADER OF JABBA'S HOUSE BAND

DATA FILE

AFFILIATION: Jabba's court
HOMEWORLD: Orto
SPECIES: Ortolan
HEIGHT: 1.5m (4ft 9in)
APPEARANCES: VI
SEE ALSO: Droopy McCool;
Sy Snootles

THE BLUE ORTOLAN, known in the entertainment business as Max Rebo, is a half-insane keyboard player who is completely obsessed with food. When the pleasure-loving crime boss Jabba the Hutt offers Max a contract that pays only in free meals, he immediately accepts—to the outrage of his bandmates!

Signed

Jabba is so enthusiastic about the wild music that the Max Rebo Band plays, he offers the band a lifetime gig at his palace. The band is playing when Luke Skywalker enters the palace to try to free Han Solo. After Jabba's death, the band breaks up.

Output speaker

Ears store fat

Air intake

Articulated toes can absorb food and drink

FOR AN

Ortolan, Max Rebo is quite skinny. His obsession with food may lead him to have poor judgment as the leader of his band, but he is devoted to music and quite good at his chosen instrument—the red ball jet organ.

Max Rebo's band accompanies Jabba's entourage on the Hutt's sail barge.

MAZ KANATA

PIRATE LEGEND

DATA FILE

AFFILIATION: Pirate; Resistance
HOMEWORLD: Takodana
SPECIES: Unknown
HEIGHT: 1.24m (4ft 1in)
APPEARANCES: VII, VIII, IX
SEE ALSO: Finn; Han Solo; Princess Leia; Rey

Variable lens corrective goggles

A MISCHIEVOUS PIRATE boss who has spent centuries surviving in the galaxy's fringe, Maz is regarded with respect by some of the toughest gangsters in space. Maz has a strong connection to the Force, but she is no Jedi. However, she does aid the Resistance's fight against the dark side of the Force.

Bracelet of the Sutro

Clothes knitted by Maz herself

MAZ'S HOSPITALITY is

legendary, and she invites independent starship crews to visit her castle keep on Takodana. As long as guests don't cause trouble, and grudges and politics are left at the door, Maz is happy to host all manner of law-bending wanderers in her home.

Scoundrel's Reunion

Han Solo has known Maz Kanata for decades, and describes her as an "acquired taste." Though she is small, Maz has a big and playful personality, passing on her wisdom with equal parts good humor and stinging criticism. Solo visits Maz after an absence of 25 years, to get help finding the Resistance. As Solo brings with him two fugitives from the First Order, evil forces close in and the Resistance soon comes to him.

ME-8D9

DATA FILE

AFFILIATION: None
TYPE: Unknown
MANUFACTURER: Unknown
HEIGHT: 1.72m (5ft 8in)
APPEARANCES: VII
SEE ALSO: Bazine Netal; Maz Kanata

KNOWN AS "Emmie" to the scoundrels within Maz's castle on Takodana, ME-8D9 is a protocol droid who is often called on to translate the less-than-legal deals made within the castle's dining and gaming halls.

Shielded data storage center

Bronzium-enriched finish

EMMIE IS an ancient droid of an unknown model, and rumor has it that she is as old as the castle itself. Emmie has little memory of her original functions, and she has been reprogrammed countless times.

Knee assembly

Reinforced ankle joint

Mysterious Past

Fragments of Emmie's past surface occasionally— a side effect of her outdated design. Though mainly built for protocol duty, she has also served as an assassin for shady criminals, including the notorious Crymorah. There are some who believe she was originally in the service of the ancient Jedi Order.

MIGS MAYFELD

SHARPSHOOTER FOR HIRE

DATA FILE

AFFILIATION: Empire;
Independent
HOMEWORLD: Unknown
SPECIES: Human
HEIGHT: 1.7m (5ft 7in)
APPEARANCES: M
SEE ALSO: Cara Dune; the
Mandalorian; Valin Hess

Multiple leather holsters
for quick access to weapons

Enhanced backpack for neuro-link pack

A neuro-link automated
weapons solution pack allows
Mayfeld to aim the weapon
with his mind.

Steady hands with fast reflexes

Rusty belt buckle

MIGS MAYFELD IS a wise-cracking criminal for hire who frequently upsets the people around him. He is smart, and an excellent marksman, but his quick temper often gets him and his companions into trouble.

Conflicted

Mayfeld is arrested and sentenced to work in the Karthon Chop Fields. New Republic Marshal Cara Dune releases him to help Mando locate Moff Gideon and the captured Grogu by sneaking into an Imperial refinery.

MAYFELD USED to be an Imperial sharpshooter, but he didn't like how the Empire treated people. He is angry that his former commander, Valin Hess, cares more about the Empire than about protecting innocent lives.

Protective spats

MOFF GIDEON

CRUEL IMPERIAL LEADER

DATA FILE

AFFILIATION: Empire;
Imperial Remnant
HOMEWORLD: Unknown
SPECIES: Human
HEIGHT: 1.83m (6ft)
APPEARANCES: M
SEE ALSO: Bo-Katan Kryze;
Grogu; the Mandalorian

Moff rank indicator

Mando's beskar spear strikes Moff Gideon's Darksaber as they duel over Grogu.

MOFF GIDEON searches
the galaxy for the Child,
Grogu. Gideon shows
no mercy to anyone
who stands in his
way—even his
own stormtroopers.

The legendary
Darksaber of
Mandalore

Ruthless

Moff Gideon holds Cara
Dune, Greef Karga, and
the Mandalorian hostage
in a cantina on Nevarro.
He wants Grogu, and
refuses to promise them
safety, even if he gets
what he wants.

FORMERLY an Imperial
Security Bureau (ISB) officer, Moff
Gideon is smart and relentless as
he leads a portion of the Imperial
Remnant. Gideon is skilled with
the Darksaber, even though he has
no Force abilities.

Leather boots

MOFF JERJERROD

SUPERVISOR OF THE SECOND DEATH STAR

DATA FILE

AFFILIATION: Empire
HOMEWORLD: Tinnel IV
SPECIES: Human
HEIGHT: 1.83m (6ft)
APPEARANCES: VI
SEE ALSO: Captain Needa;
Darth Vader

MOFF JERJERROD SUPERVISES the construction of the second Death Star. During the Battle of Endor, Jerjerrod commands the station's superlaser against the rebel forces. He is killed when the rebels finally detonate the Death Star's reactor.

Imperial code cylinder

Rank insignia plaque

Imperial officer's tunic

Jerjerrod blames slow progress of the Death Star's construction on a shortfall of workers.

Naval boots

JERJERROD was born to a wealthy family on the Core World of Tinnel IV. He shows petty spitefulness and a lack of ambition as he rises through the Imperial ranks—both admirable qualities in a Moff. When he is assigned to the top-secret second Death Star project, his cover title is Director of Imperial Energy Systems.

Called to Account

When the construction of the Death Star falls behind schedule, the Emperor sends Vader to put additional pressure on Moff Jerjerrod and his construction crews. Informed that the Emperor himself will soon be arriving, Jerjerrod assures Vader his men will double their efforts.

MOLOCH

WHITE WORMS ENFORCER

DATA FILE

AFFILIATION: White Worms
HOMEWORLD: Corellia
SPECIES: Grindalid
HEIGHT: 2m (6ft 7in)
APPEARANCES: S
SEE ALSO: Han Solo; Lady Proxima; Qi'ra

Mask protects skin from sunlight

A BRUTISH Grindalid named Moloch is an enforcer for Lady Proxima and her gang, the White Worms. The Grindalids run the black market in Coronet City and eat a diet of rats brought to them by their network of underlings.

Scepter decorated with writhing scrumrats

Resourceful scrumrats who prove to be useful can be promoted to engage in more serious crime.

Salt-encrusted clothes from wet, briny throne room

MOST GRINDALIDS

stay hidden away in their den because Corellia's sun burns their skin, but Moloch ventures outside. He wears long clothes and a mask so every part of his body is covered. He has also trained himself to move on his tail as though he has human legs.

Loyal Servant

Moloch serves his "dear matriarch," Lady Proxima. She leads the criminal gang that runs a horde of human "scrumrats," who are desperate children forced to catch rats for her hatchlings, pick pocket and commit other petty crimes. Han Solo and Qi'ra began their criminal careers as scrumrats.

MON MOTHMA

REBEL ALLIANCE LEADER

DATA FILE

AFFILIATION: Republic; Rebel Alliance; New Republic
HOMEWORLD: Chandrila
SPECIES: Human
HEIGHT: 1.73m (5ft 8in)
APPEARANCES: III, RO, VI
SEE ALSO: Bail Organa

Simple Chandrilan hairstyle

Hanna pendant

Elegant robe of Fleuréline weave

Gesture of reconciliation

MON MOTHMA IS THE highest leader of the Rebellion. As a member of the Galactic Senate, she champions the cause of freedom until the Emperor's evil closes in around her. Abandoning the Senate, Mothma works with Bail Organa to form the Rebel Alliance that aims to unseat the Galactic Empire.

Mon Mothma listens to all the opinions on the Rebel Council about the alleged Death Star.

Shraa silk mantle

Rebel Founders

Mon Mothma and Bail Organa become convinced that Palpatine needs to be opposed. With the Senate under Palpatine's control, and his newly appointed governors overseeing all star systems, the two loyalists make a pact with a few dependable Senators to form a highly secret Rebellion movement.

MON MOTHMA was born into a political family and became the youngest senator to enter the Senate. When the Republic collapses, she goes underground and begins to organize the various cells of resistance into a single entity: The Alliance to Restore the Republic (or Rebel Alliance).

MORGAN ELSBETH

CRUEL TYRANT

MORGAN ELSBETH is the ruler of Calodan, a city on the planet Corvus. Elsbeth is at odds with Ahsoka Tano, after the magistrate refuses to tell the former Jedi the location of her master, Grand Admiral Thrawn.

Beskar spear

MORGAN ELSBETH

used to strip worlds of resources to help build the Imperial Navy. She continues to conquer planets after the Empire's fall.

Utility belt with hidden rope

Deadly Deal

Morgan hires the Mandalorian, Din Djarin, to defeat Tano. As payment, she offers Djarin a spear made of pure beskar—an almost indestructible metal used by Mandalorians.

Magistrate's robe

Ahsoka Tano defends herself from Elsbeth's strike inside Calodan's walls.

MUDTROOPER

IMPERIAL SWAMP TROOPERS

DATA FILE

AFFILIATION: Empire
HOMEWORLD: Various
SPECIES: Human
HEIGHT: Varies
STANDARD EQUIPMENT:
E-10 blaster rifle
APPEARANCES: S
SEE ALSO: Han Solo;
Tobias Beckett

THE IMPERIAL ARMY relies on regular troops alongside its stormtroopers. On the swampy planet of Mimban, mudtroopers of the 244th Imperial Armored Division are caught in a quagmire, fighting local Mimbanese guerillas.

Respirator mask for hazardous air

Waterproof capes nicknamed "slicks"

Han is sent to Mimban after being expelled from the Imperial pilot academy.

Camp Forward

Conditions on misty, swampy Mimban are harsh. Aside from the local insurgency threat, there is the risk of trench foot from the marshy ground and lung disease from fungal spores in the air. Mudtroopers cannot even drink vaporated water because it contains harmful microbes.

FEW CHOOSE the life of a mudtrooper. Most of the soldiers on Mimban were conscripted. However, some were sent as punishment for insubordination in other parts of the army, and a few agreed to serve there in exchange for a military scholarship.

NABOO GUARD

BODYGUARD OF THE NABOO MONARCHY

DATA FILE

AFFILIATION: Naboo Royal Security Forces
HOMEWORLD: Naboo
SPECIES: Human
HEIGHT: Varies
STANDARD EQUIPMENT: S-5 blaster pistol, comlink
APPEARANCES: I, II
SEE ALSO: Captain Panaka

THE NABOO ROYAL GUARD is the highly trained bodyguard of the Naboo monarch and court. Its loyal, dedicated soldiers typically experience battle offworld and return to Naboo to protect the royal house out of loyalty.

No leg armor for mobility

THE ROYAL GUARD forms one component of the Naboo Royal Security Forces. Its members work alongside the Security Guard, which comprises mainly sentries and patrolmen, and the Naboo Space Fighter Corps, which flies N-1 starfighters.

Shin protectors

Naboo forces use small Gian landspeeders in their attempt to repel the invading droid army.

Blast-damping armor

Unarmored joints for agility

Utility belt

Returning Forces

When the Trade Federation droid army invades Naboo, the Royal Guard gets its first taste of true battle. But the sheer number of battle droids means a defeat for Naboo. Fortunately, Queen Amidala and the Head of Security, Captain Panaka, escape and are able to return, with the Gungans, to put an end to the droid occupation.

NAMBI GHIMA

FRIENDLY JUVENILE

DATA FILE

AFFILIATION: Aki-Aki
HOMEWORLD: Pasaana
SPECIES: Aki-Aki
HEIGHT: 1.3m (4ft 3in)
APPEARANCES: IX
SEE ALSO: C-3PO; Rey

Daswoad-dyed fabric

Short trunk is a
sign of youth

Necklace made
from kern-nut husks

NAMBI GHIMA is a young
Aki-Aki celebrating the
Festival of the Ancestors
with her people on
Pasaana. The event
celebrates Aki-Aki
history and their future.
Nambi offers Rey a
necklace as a gift
to welcome her.

Nambi Ghima asks Rey what
her family name is, with help
from protocol droid C-3PO.

Loose robes for dancing

THE FESTIVAL of the
Ancestors takes place on Pasaana
every 42 years. Most of the attendees
are local Aki-Aki, but some offworlders
seek the festival out to enjoy the music
and dancing as well as the sweets and
crafts for sale.

Force Connection
The Force connects Rey and Kylo
Ren shortly after she speaks to Nambi. Ren
angrily grabs Rey's necklace even though
they are physically far apart. The First
Order tracks her whereabouts to Pasaana
by examining the necklace's beads.

NIEN NUNB

HEROIC SULLUSTAN PILOT

DATA FILE

AFFILIATION: Rebel Alliance; Resistance
HOMEWORLD: Sullust
SPECIES: Sullustan
HEIGHT: 1.79m (5ft 10in)
APPEARANCES: VI, VII, VIII, IX
SEE ALSO: Lando Calrissian; Poe Dameron; Princess Leia

NIEN NUNB is Lando Calrissian's Sullustan copilot on board the *Millennium Falcon* at the Battle of Endor. Lando understands the Sullustan language that Nunb speaks, and personally picks him for the mission, impressed by Nunb's exploits aboard his own renowned vessel, the *Mellcrawler*.

Tool pouch

Pressurized g-suit

Flight gauntlets

Gear harness

NIEN NUNB is one of many Sullustans who serve as fighter pilots in the Rebel Alliance. His homeworld, Sullust, is the staging area for the rebel fleet before the Battle of Endor. The Alliance awards Nunb a medal named the Kalidor Crescent for his bravery in the battle.

Nunb serves in the depleted Resistance fleet. He survives D'Qar and Crait, but dies during the Battle of Exegol.

Positive-grip boots

Trusted Pilot

Nunb learned his piloting skills flying a freighter for the Sullustan SoroSuub Corporation. When SoroSuub begins to support the Empire, Nunb shows his opposition by stealing from the company on behalf of the Rebel Alliance. At first, Nunb works as an independent smuggler, but he eventually becomes a full-time member of the Alliance.

NUTE GUNRAY

NEIMOIDIAN VICEROY

DATA FILE

AFFILIATION: Trade Federation; Separatists
HOMEWORLD: Neimoidia
SPECIES: Neimoidian
HEIGHT: 1.91m (6ft 3in)
APPEARANCES: I, II, III
SEE ALSO: Padmé Amidala; Palpatine

Viceroy's crested tiara

Wheedling expression

Viceroy's collar

THE VICEROY OF THE Trade Federation, Nute Gunray, is powerful, deceitful, and willing to kill for his far-reaching commercial aims. Gunray becomes an unwitting pawn of Darth Sidious when he agrees to invade the peaceful planet of Naboo.

The Trade Federation secretly aids the Separatists during the Clone Wars.

Sidious will need the Trade Federation's help only until his control of the galaxy is assured.

NUTE GUNRAY

is a Neimoidian, a species known for its exceptional greed. Gunray makes an alliance with Darth Sidious to blockade Naboo in opposition to increased taxation. However, Gunray feels increasingly uneasy when his alliance with Sidious leads to open warfare.

True Face

Gunray's true cowardice shows itself when Padmé Amidala's freedom fighters storm the Royal Palace. Unable to hide behind battle droids any longer, Gunray is arrested. It is a sign of the Republic's decay that he is later able to buy his release and continue as Viceroy of the Trade Federation.

OBI-WAN KENOBI

LEGENDARY JEDI MASTER

DATA FILE

AFFILIATION: Jedi
HOMEWORLD: Stewjon
SPECIES: Human
HEIGHT: 1.79m (5ft 10in)
APPEARANCES: I, II, III, IV, V, VI
SEE ALSO: Anakin Skywalker; Luke Skywalker

Under-tunic

Jedi robe

Kenobi faces Darth Vader—known previously as his Padawan, Anakin Skywalker—in battle.

OBI-WAN KENOBI is a truly great Jedi who finds himself at the heart of galactic turmoil as the Republic unravels and finally collapses. Although cautious by nature, Kenobi has a healthy independent streak and truly formidable lightsaber skills.

KENOBI'S PATH

is destined to lead in a very different direction to that of his apprentice, Anakin Skywalker. After Order 66, Kenobi helps protect Luke Skywalker and Leia Organa. For many years, he hides on Tatooine, watching over young Luke, the last hope for the ancient Jedi Order.

General Kenobi

Kenobi becomes a great Jedi General and pilot in the Clone Wars (despite his reluctance to fly). Trained by the headstrong Qui-Gon Jinn, Kenobi trains his own master's protégé, Anakin Skywalker, after Jinn's death. The bond between Kenobi and Anakin is strong as they fight through the Clone Wars.

Kenobi's considered approach to situations often conflicts with Anakin's brash nature.

OCHI OF BESTOON

SITH ASSASSIN

DATA FILE

AFFILIATION: Acolytes of the Beyond; Sith Eternal
HOMEWORLD: Unknown
SPECIES: Unknown
HEIGHT: 1.83m (6ft)
APPEARANCES: IX
SEE ALSO: C-3PO; D-O; Palpatine; Rey

Cybernetic headgear

OCHI OF BESTOON is a fabled hunter of Sith artifacts who also serves Darth Sidious as an assassin. Although Ochi does not use the Force, he believes it guides him. He dies in the lethal quicksands on Pasaana.

Wrist-mounted communication device

THE SECRET CULT

known as the Sith Eternal sends Ochi to find Palpatine's granddaughter Rey. When Rey's parents refuse to give up her location, Ochi kills them. Later, the Sith runes on Ochi's blade help lead the Resistance to Palpatine.

Wears cape in stylistic nod to dark-side traditions

Ochi's Ship

Ochi gets trapped in the sinking fields on Pasaana and is unable to return to his ship, the *Bestoon Legacy*, where his droid D-O remains. Poe Dameron commandeers the ship for a daring rescue mission to a First Order Star Destroyer.

Ochi is one of the Acolytes of the Beyond, who believe the Sith are destined to return to power.

OMERA

MOTHER AND PROTECTOR

DATA FILE

AFFILIATION: Unknown
HOMEWORLD: Sorgan
SPECIES: Human
HEIGHT: 1.73m (5ft 8in)
APPEARANCES: M
SEE ALSO: Grogu; the Mandalorian; Winta

OMERA LIVES ON the planet Sorgan with her daughter, Winta. She wants to keep Winta safe, and leads her fellow villagers in their preparations to defend against invaders. She is caring and brave, and willing to fight for what she loves.

Decorative collar

Ruffled sleeves for comfort

OMERA AND Winta live peacefully in a village of krill farmers until a group of raiders vandalizes their village. When the Mandalorian offers his help, she becomes friends with him and invites him into her home.

Large skirt made from local fibers

Omera and Winta hide from Klatooinian raiders.

Ready For The Fight

Mando trains Omera to defend her village. He is impressed by Omera's survival instinct and her skill with a blaster, and realizes she is more than a match for any enemy.

Waterproof waders

OOLA

TWI'LEK DANCER

DATA FILE

AFFILIATION: Jabba's court
HOMEWORLD: Ryloth
SPECIES: Twi'lek
HEIGHT: 1.6m (5ft 3in)
APPEARANCES: VI
SEE ALSO: Jabba the Hutt

OOLA IS A green-skinned Twi'lek dancer enslaved to the cruel crime lord Jabba the Hutt. Jabba's majordomo, Bib Fortuna, kidnapped Oola from her clan. He had other Twi'leks train Oola to dance, and forces her to perform for Jabba.

Lekku (head-tail)

Leather straps

Oola ends up in the dreaded rancor pit.

Flimsy net costume

OOLA'S LIFE is tragic and short. Enslaved by Bib Fortuna, a stranger offers her the chance to escape in Mos Eisley. However, Fortuna has fed her so many lies about the glory of Jabba's palace that she wants to see it for herself, so she refuses this opportunity to be free.

Gruesome End

Jabba lavishes particular attention on Oola, keeping her chained to his throne. However, Oola refuses Jabba's advances, and the revolting Hutt is infuriated. He opens the trap door beneath the dance floor, dropping Oola into a pit with his deadly pet rancor.

OPPO RANCISIS

JEDI HIGH COUNCIL MEMBER

DATA FILE

AFFILIATION: Jedi
HOMEWORLD: Thisspias
SPECIES: Thisspiasian
LENGTH: 5.49m (18ft)
APPEARANCES: I, II
SEE ALSO: Yaddle

OPPO RANCISIS IS a Thisspiasian Jedi Master who has served the Jedi Council since the days of the High Republic. He joined the Jedi Order as an infant and trained under Master Yaddle. When offered the throne of Thisspias, he declined it to continue to serve the galaxy as a Jedi. He is now a top Jedi military advisor.

Dense hair deters biting cygnats of Thisspias

RANCISIS IS an excellent strategist, who ensures that, if negotiation fails, Jedi-counseled military tactics are cunning and effective. During the Clone Wars, Rancisis fights in the Siege of Saleucami, but also spends much time on Coruscant, coordinating Republic forces throughout the galaxy. He is rumored to survive Order 66.

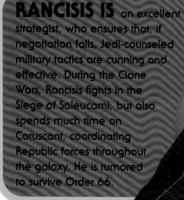

Second pair of hands hidden underneath cloak

Master Jedi

Rancisis is adept with his green-bladed lightsaber, but prefers to use his highly developed Force powers for combat. He is a formidable foe in unarmed combat, using his four arms and long tail to make surprising strikes at his opponent.

Fingers tipped with claws

ORSON KRENNIC

DIRECTOR OF WEAPONS RESEARCH

DATA FILE

AFFILIATION: Empire
HOMEWORLD: Lexrul
SPECIES: Human
HEIGHT: 1.8m (5ft 11in)
APPEARANCES: RO
SEE ALSO: Galen Erso;
Grand Moff Tarkin; Jyn Erso;
Saw Gerrera

A DIRECTOR of the Empire's Advanced Weapons Research Division, Orson Krennic heads up the Tarkin Initiative—the think tank responsible for creating the Death Star. He reached this exalted position thanks to his scientific mind and ruthless ambition.

Rank plaque shows the equivalent of Admiral

Coded key cylinder

DT-29 heavy blaster pistol

KRENNIC'S THIRST

for power knows no bounds, but working for the Imperial leadership is precarious. Even after a successful test shot on Jedha, Orson is grateful to leave his encounter with Darth Vader with his job and his life.

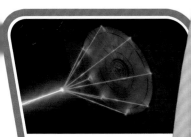

On seeing the awe-inspiring capacity of kyber crystals, Krennic's first thought is to weaponize them.

Science at any Cost

Krennic sees the devastating potential in Galen Erso's research while they are science colleagues. When Erso does not share Krennic's vision, the cruel Imperial agent has no qualms about capturing Erso, destroying his family, and forcing him to work under duress.

OWEN LARS

LUKE SKYWALKER'S GUARDIAN

DATA FILE

AFFILIATION: None
HOMEWORLD: Tatooine
SPECIES: Human
HEIGHT: 1.7m (5ft 6in)
APPEARANCES: II, III, IV
SEE ALSO: Beru Lars; Cliegg Lars; Luke Skywalker

AS A YOUNG NEWLYWED, Owen Lars made a huge decision. He agreed to hide and protect a baby from the wrath of his own father: Darth Vader. The baby was named Luke by his mother, Padmé, moments before she died in childbirth. Owen gained a nephew, but also added to his worries.

Rough clothing made in Anchorhead

Simple overcoat provides warmth in the cold desert evenings

Tool pouch

YOUNG OWEN was born to Cliegg Lars and his first wife, Aika. He has spent most of his life on his father's homestead on Tatooine, which he inherited after Cliegg passed away. Owen falls in love with Beru after meeting her in nearby Anchorhead. It is Beru who convinces the reluctant Owen to adopt Anakin's son.

A Farmer's Life

When Luke has grown up, he works closely with Owen on the family homestead. They maintain the vaporators that collect precious moisture from the desert air, and buy "used" droids from passing Jawas. Although the teenage Luke is ready to fly the nest, Owen finds it hard to shrug off the gruff, protective attitude that has become a habit over the years.

Owen, his wife, Beru, and father Cliegg met Luke's parents, Anakin and Padmé, only once.

PADMÉ AMIDALA

NABOO QUEEN AND SENATOR

DATA FILE

AFFILIATION: Royal House of Naboo, Galactic Senate
HOMEWORLD: Naboo
SPECIES: Human
HEIGHT: 1.65m (5ft 4in)
APPEARANCES: I, II, III
SEE ALSO: Anakin Skywalker; Captain Panaka; Sabé

Hair pulled tightly back for clear view of enemy

TIME AND AGAIN Padmé Amidala has been at the very center of galactic events. From the invasion of her home planet, Naboo, to a death sentence in a Geonosian arena, by way of multiple attempts on her life as a senator, Padmé faces extraordinary danger with determination and great bravery.

Utility belt

PADMÉ GREW

up in a small Naboo village. Exceptionally talented, she was elected queen at the age of only 14. At the end of her term of office, Padmé is made senator of Naboo. It is in this role, on the Galactic capital, Coruscant, that she becomes closer to Anakin Skywalker.

Light shin armor

Queen Turned Fighter

As the young Queen of Naboo, Padmé Amidala has to learn that her cherished values of nonviolence will not save her people from a brutal droid invasion. Discarding her formal robes of state, Padmé determines to inspire her own troops to end the invasion by capturing the Neimoidian leaders.

Padmé and Anakin surrender to the love they share, though they know it breaks Jedi rules.

Action boots with firm grip

PAIGE TICO

RESISTANCE BOMBER

Tight-fitting
flight cap

Atmosphere hose

Buoyancy
foam-filled
flight vest collar

PAIGE TICO and her sister, Rose, have always done everything together, including joining the Resistance. They hope to see the galaxy one day, but for now Paige is a Resistance pilot, with many successful missions under her belt.

AS THE VENTRAL

gunner, Paige usually flies in a rotating ball turret under the bomb racks, firing repeating laser cannons. Pilots can be superstitious, and Paige is no exception. She sometimes wraps a medallion around the struts of her cannons. Her sister holds the other half.

Resistance Hero

At D'Qar, the Resistance has the rare chance to take out a First Order Dreadnought, but all hope seems lost when no one can trigger the bombs. With all her might, Paige manages to release the 1,048 proton bombs. She cannot save herself, but the *Fulminatrix's* destruction enables the rest of the Resistance to escape.

Paige flies in the *Cobalt Hammer*, an MG-100 StarFortress bomber, in the Cobalt Squadron.

PALPATINE

SITH LORD AND GALACTIC EMPEROR

DATA FILE

AFFILIATION: Sith; Republic; Empire; Sith Eternal
HOMEWORLD: Naboo
SPECIES: Human
HEIGHT: 1.78m (5ft 10in)
APPEARANCES: I, II, III, V, VI, IX
SEE ALSO: Darth Vader

Hood to hide face

Palpatine secretly plans the Clone Wars to destroy the Galactic Republic and the Jedi Order.

PALPATINE is known by many names. Born on Naboo, Sheev Palpatine becomes his homeworld's senator. Then, he is Supreme Chancellor Palpatine. Finally, he declares himself Emperor and rules the galaxy. Ultimate power has been his plan all along. He is secretly Darth Sidious, the most evil of Sith Lords.

PALPATINE manages to keep all those around him from suspecting his true identity. For years, he has appeared patient and unassuming, so few have recognized his political ambitions. His dark side powers even blinded the Jedi from seeing behind his mask of affability.

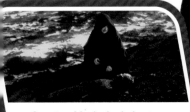

Sensing Vader's defeat on Mustafar, Palpatine travels to his apprentice's side.

Sith Eternal

With the help of loyal Sith cultists, Palpatine is able to live on as a clone after his apparent death on the second Death Star. His condition, however, is weak, and he must use forbidden medical science to survive. He seeks out Rey in order to take her power and return to rule the galaxy once more.

PAO

FIERCE REBEL COMMANDO

DATA FILE

AFFILIATION: Rebel Alliance
HOMEWORLD: Pipada
SPECIES: Drabatan
HEIGHT: 1.72m (5ft 8in)
APPEARANCES: RO
SEE ALSO:
Bistan

Antenna on backpack

PAO IS A soldier with the Rebel Alliance Special Forces. In battle, you hear him coming before you see him. Drabatans have booming voices, and Pao puts his to good use with a blood-chilling war cry.

Black-market blaster

External tibanna gas chamber

PAO IS AN explosives expert who has also studied structural engineering. He specializes in demolitions, particularly underwater. As an amphibian, he can thrive on both land and in the water, though he prefers freshwater to the salty seawater of Scarif.

Pao's thirst for battle is exceeded only by his hatred of the Empire.

Water-shedding fatigues

Fearless Fighter

Pao is quick to volunteer for the rogue mission to Scarif as part of the historic team who retrieve the Death Star plans. While Jyn Erso and Cassian Andor sneak into the Citadel Tower, Pao and his squad are tasked with causing a distraction on the ground and making 10 soldiers look like 100.

PATROL TROOPER

CORONET CITY POLICE

Enlarged helmets have improved visual displays

DATA FILE

AFFILIATION: Empire
HOMEWORLD: Various
SPECIES: Human
HEIGHT (AVG.): 1.83m (6ft)
STANDARD EQUIPMENT: C-PH patrol speeder bike; EC-17 hold-out blasters
APPEARANCES: S
SEE ALSO: Scout Trooper

AS THE EMPIRE tightens its grip on new worlds, it replaces local defense forces with its own specialist military law enforcement agencies. Patrol troopers are the Imperial answer to stormtrooper city policing.

Fabric gives legs more flexibility than armor

A patrol trooper fails to catch Han Solo and Qi'ra, who are speeding through Coronet City.

PATROL TROOPERS

are the urban equivalent of scout troopers, who are deployed in wilderness areas like the Moon of Endor. They cruise city streets maintaining law and order. Like scout troopers, they wear protective helmets and chest armor, but stop short of full stormtrooper armor.

City Speeders

On Corellia, patrol troopers ride C-PH patrol speeder bikes. These chunky, single-rider bikes are small enough to maneuver in tight spots, but also robust in a collision. Patrol troopers receive real-time highway intel to avoid the worst traffic.

PAZ VIZSLA

HEAVY-GUNNER MANDALORIAN

DATA FILE

AFFILIATION: Mandalorians
HOMEWORLD: Mandalore
SPECIES: Human
HEIGHT: 1.91m
(6ft 3in)
APPEARANCES: M
SEE ALSO: The
Armorer; Grogu;
the Mandalorian

Infrared
scope

SHORT-TEMPERED and
proud, Paz Vizsla lives
on Nevarro with a small
group of Mandalorians
and fights to preserve
their history and traditions.
He hates the Empire and
anyone who works
with them, no matter
the reason.

Heavy reinforced chest plate

Flamethrower

PAZ VIZSLA starts a
fight with the Mandalorian when
he learns Mando received
Imperial beskar. He is calmed
by the Armorer, who defends
Mando, saying those who choose
the Mandalorian Way cannot be
questioned or called cowards.

Blue beskar armor

Gravity stabilizer
for flight balance

Paz Vizsla and Mando
debate what it means to
honor the traditions of the
warriors of Mandalore.

To The Rescue

A group of Mandalorians, led by
Paz Vizsla, use their jetpacks to fly
to the Mandalorian's rescue so he
can help Grogu escape bounty
hunters. Paz uses a heavy-
repeating blaster to provide
cover for his companion.

PELI MOTTO

MOS EISLEY MECHANIC

TATOOINE MECHANIC with a temper Peli Motto works with pit droids and specializes in fixing and refueling ships that land in her hangar. She speaks her mind and is brutally honest, but is also kind and compassionate to those who need help.

Wide-bore donderbus blaster rifle

Droid caller attached to tool belt

Satchels containing diagnostic scanner and other gadgets

AN EXCELLENT judge of character, Peli Motto introduces the Mandalorian to Frog Lady so that Mando can help her. She believes Mando should take Frog Lady to meet her husband and save their family line from extinction.

Idiot's Array

Inside the cantina in Mos Eisley, Peli Motto plays a game of sabacc. She is a skilled player and beats her opponent with the game's best hand, known as the Idiot's Array.

Grogu and Peli Motto become fast friends, and Peli agrees to watch over the cute little alien.

Work overalls

PLO KOON

JEDI HIGH COUNCIL MEMBER

Antiox mask

Thick hide covers body

Loose Jedi cloak

Plo Koon's starfighter crashes into a city on the Neimoidian planet of Cato Neimoidia.

PLO KOON is a member of the Jedi High Council and a Jedi General in the Clone Wars. He is one of the most powerful Jedi ever, with awesome fighting abilities and strong telekinetic powers. He also discovered Ahsoka Tano as an infant and inducted her into the Jedi Order.

PLO KOON is a Kel Dor from Dorin. He wears a special mask to protect his sensitive eyes and nostrils from the oxygen-rich atmosphere of planets such as Coruscant. Master Plo Koon fights in the Battle of Geonosis and many more conflicts in the Clone Wars.

Tragic Mission

At the end of the Clone Wars, Plo Koon, an expert pilot, leads a starfighter patrol in Cato Neimoidia's atmosphere. Without warning, his own clone troopers begin firing at his ship. Order 66 had been given, causing all the pre-programmed clones to turn on their Jedi leaders. Plo Koon's ship crashes into the planet, and he is killed.

Practical combat/flight boots

POE DAMERON

BEST PILOT IN THE GALAXY

DATA FILE

AFFILIATION: Resistance
HOMEWORLD: Yavin 4
SPECIES: Human
HEIGHT: 1.75m (5ft 9in)
APPEARANCES: VII, VIII, IX
SEE ALSO: BB-8; Finn;
Princess Leia; Rey; Zorii Bliss

Poe's reunion with Zorii Bliss
on Kijimi is bittersweet.

AN INCREDIBLY skilled
starfighter pilot, Poe Dameron
is a commander in the
Resistance's fight against the
First Order. He soars into
battle as Black Leader,
behind the controls of
a specially modified
T-70 X-wing.

Insulated flight suit

POE GREW UP

hearing legends of the
fighter pilots of the Rebel
Alliance from his
mother, Shara Bey,
who flew an A-wing
during the Battle of
Endor. Poe's father
was Kes Dameron,
a Rebel Alliance
Pathfinder soldier.

Glie-44 blaster

Rebellious Rebel

Poe displays his fearless flying over D'Qar. In a
single, lightweight starfighter, he gets right up to
the First Order dreadnought the *Fulminatrix* and
takes out its surface cannons. Then he is reckless.
Disobeying orders to disengage, he continues to
lead the charge to bring down the ship, but at
the cost of the Resistance's whole bomber fleet.

POGGLE THE LESSER

GEONOSIAN ARCHDUKE

DATA FILE

AFFILIATION: Separatists
HOMEWORLD: Geonosis
SPECIES: Geonosian
HEIGHT: 1.83m (6ft)
APPEARANCES: II, III
SEE ALSO:
Count Dooku;
Geonosian
soldier

THE ARCHDUKE OF GEONOSIS, Poggle the Lesser, rules the Stalgasin hive colony, which controls all the other major hive colonies on Geonosis. His factories build innumerable battle droids for the Separatists, using the labor of legions of downtrodden drones.

Long wattles

POGGLE emerged from a lower caste through the sheer force of his iron will to become Archduke. He is the public face of the Geonosian aristocracy and arms business. Hidden beneath the hives of his planet is his monarch, Karina the Great, an enormous Geonosian queen whose vast egg chambers propagate the species.

High-caste wings

Aristocratic adornments

Command staff

Commissioned to design a superweapon, Poggle hands the plans to Count Dooku.

Presiding Leaders

Poggle the Lesser presides over the first meeting of the Separatist leadership on his planet, as well as the trial of Anakin Skywalker, Obi-Wan Kenobi, and Padmé Amidala, who are accused of spying. Poggle and the other Separatists take refuge in the underlevels when Republic forces arrive.

PONDA BABA

AQUALISH THUG

Large eyes for seeing underwater on native planet

DATA FILE

AFFILIATION: Smuggler
HOMEWORLD: Ando
SPECIES: Aqualish
HEIGHT: 1.7m (5ft 7in)
APPEARANCES: RO, IV
SEE ALSO: Doctor Evazan; Obi-Wan Kenobi

PONDA BABA is a thuggish Aqualish who tries to pick a fight with Luke Skywalker when Luke enters a notorious Mos Eisley cantina with Obi-Wan Kenobi looking for a ride offworld. Ponda Baba's big mistake is picking on the companion of a Jedi.

Facial tusks grow with age

TOGETHER, Ponda Baba and Doctor Evazan ship spice for Jabba the Hutt. After the fight in the cantina, Evazan tries to use his medical training to reattach Ponda Baba's arm but fails, nearly killing the Aqualish in the process.

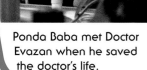

Ponda Baba met Doctor Evazan when he saved the doctor's life.

Cantina Confrontation

Ponda Baba and his partner in crime, Dr. Evazan, are caught unprepared for an old man's ability with a lightsaber as the Jedi severs Ponda's right arm from his body. But for Luke, too, this first demonstration of Kenobi's abilities with the weapon is a revelation, and a hint of the possible return of the Jedi.

PRAETORIAN GUARD

SNOKE'S LAST LINE OF DEFENSE

DATA FILE

AFFILIATION: First Order
HOMEWORLD: Unknown
SPECIES: Human
HEIGHT: Varies
STANDARD EQUIPMENT: Bilari electro-chain whip; electro-bisento; twin vibro-arbir blades; vibro-voulge
APPEARANCES: VIII
SEE ALSO: Kylo Ren; Supreme Leader Snoke

Segmented armor plates

Twin vibro-arbir blades

Ever vigilant, the guards are ready to leap into action against Snoke's many enemies.

THE PRAETORIAN Guard are eight sentries who stand in Supreme Leader Snoke's throne room aboard the *Supremacy*. They act as his elite bodyguards.

THE RED clothing worn by Praetorian Guards harks back to the robes worn by Emperor Palpatine's Royal Guard. But these uniforms have been upgraded to be robust armor, able to deflect even blaster fire.

Armorweave robes

Elegant Terror

These warriors battle in a unique martial-art style with vibrating melee weapons that bristle with electro-plasma energy. However, they have never been truly tested against those with formidable Force powers.

PRINCESS LEIA

GENERAL OF THE RESISTANCE

DATA FILE

AFFILIATION: Rebel Alliance; Resistance
HOMEWORLD: Alderaan
SPECIES: Human
HEIGHT: 1.55m (5ft 1in)
APPEARANCES: III, RO, IV, V, VI, VII, VIII, IX
SEE ALSO: Bail Organa; Han Solo; Luke Skywalker

AS SENATOR for Alderaan, Princess Leia Organa made diplomatic missions across the galaxy on her ship, the *Tantive IV*. Secretly, Leia worked for the Rebel Alliance, and she played a vital role in the defeat of the Empire.

Resistance uniform

RAISED ON Alderaan by her adoptive father, Bail Organa, Leia was well prepared for her royal position, and used her high-placed connections wherever she could to aid the Alliance. During the decades of peace that follow the destruction of the Empire, Leia is able to focus on her political career and her new family, but as the galaxy once again undergoes turmoil, she returns to her role as a military commander.

Decisive Leader

Leia was a key command figure in the Rebel Alliance, overseeing important missions and planning strategy, alongside General Rieekan and other Alliance leaders. In Echo Base on Hoth, Leia peered intently at the scanners, alert to any signs of Imperial detection.

Travel boots

Leia trains as a Jedi under her brother Luke Skywalker after the Battle of Endor.

PZ-4CO

COMMUNICATIONS DROID

DATA FILE

AFFILIATION: Resistance
TYPE: Communications droid
MANUFACTURER:
Serv-O-Droid
HEIGHT: 2.06m (6ft 9in)
APPEARANCES: VII, VIII
SEE ALSO: Admiral Statura;
C-3PO; Lieutenant Connix;
Princess Leia

Elongated
neck

Data storage center

Intermotor
actuating coupler

Fine manipulators

A CONSTANT FIXTURE in
the Resistance base control
rooms, PZ-4CO offers tactical
data and communications
support during important
operations. She speaks in
a pleasant, soothing voice.

THE PREVALENCE

of humanoid species in the
galaxy has helped shape the
forms of most protocol droids,
as they are designed to mimic
the life forms they interact
with. PZ-4CO's anatomy is
specifically modeled on the
long-necked Tofallid species.

Intelligence Droids

PZ-4CO is one of many droids that form
an invisible Resistance intelligence
network. Droid agents scattered across
the galaxy transmit reports back to
Resistance headquarters, which
PZ-4CO and C-3PO then assess in
order to paint a real-time picture
of First Order movements.

Q9-0

CRIMINAL PROTOCOL DROID

Communications antenna

DATA FILE

AFFILIATION: Ranzar Malk's crew
TYPE: Protocol droid
MANUFACTURER: Unknown
HEIGHT: 1.8m (5ft 11in)
APPEARANCES: M
SEE ALSO: Frog Lady; Ranzar Malk; Xi'an

Frog Lady hacks into Q9-0's vocabulator in order to communicate with Din Djarin.

Bug-like photoreceptors behind mirrored domes

Recharge port

Vambrace

Pockets containing blaster repairs

MODIFIED PROTOCOL droid Q9-0 pilots the *Razor Crest* during a mission with Ran Malk's crew. Q9-0 considers his intellect and mechanical abilities to be superior to those of humans, or "organics," and is quick to share that knowledge with those around him.

Q9-0 IS frequently called "Zero" by his acquaintances. Zero's programming allows him to execute complicated piloting maneuvers that are impossible for humans to duplicate.

Risk Assessment

Q9-0 attempts to kill Grogu shortly after playing a holographic message from Greef Karga—interpreting Grogu's bounty to be a priority. Din Djarin returns to the ship just in time to save Grogu by blasting Q9-0 to pieces.

QI'RA

CRIMSON DAWN LIEUTENANT

DATA FILE

AFFILIATION: Crimson Dawn
HOMEWORLD: Corellia
SPECIES: Human
HEIGHT: 1.58m (5ft 2in)
APPEARANCES: S
SEE ALSO: Dryden Vos;
Han Solo; Maul

QI'RA HAS COME a long way. Once a poor street urchin and scrumrat in the White Worms gang with Han Solo, she is now the right-hand lieutenant of the notorious crime boss Dryden Vos.

Moof-leather jacket with voorpak-fur lining

To get into the Kessel mines in a ploy to steal coaxium, Qi'ra pretends to be a slave trader.

HER INFLUENTIAL position with Dryden Vos serves Qi'ra well, but working for Crimson Dawn is not a safe occupation. She navigates its dangerous waters with cunning and ruthlessness. Many have overlooked Qi'ra, unaware of her highly strategic mind and Teräs Käsi combat skills. Meanwhile, she patiently watches, listens, and waits.

Underestimated

Qi'ra kills Dryden Vos, and with him the shackles that tie her to Crimson Dawn. However, rather than making her escape, she reveals her true ambitions. She takes Vos' place in the organization with cool calculation, and reports directly to Maul.

QIN

TWI'LEK MERCENARY

DATA FILE

AFFILIATION: Ranzar Malk's crew
HOMEWORLD: Ryloth
SPECIES: Twi'lek
HEIGHT: 1.8m (5ft 11in)
APPEARANCES: M
SEE ALSO: Ranzar Malk; the Mandalorian; Xi'an

Lekku

HOT-TEMPERED TWI'LEK Qin waits in a New Republic cell, labeled prisoner X-6-9-11, following a failed mission with Ranzar Malk's crew. Qin blames the Mandalorian Din Djarin for leaving him behind and so adds him to his list of enemies.

Clenched fists reveal frustration

Worker's gloves

A TWI'LEK'S SKIN

color can be a variety of shades including purple, blue, green, pink, orange, red, and yellow. Most Twi'leks have two lekku but some, such as politician Orn Free Taa, have four. Twi'leks strengthen their lekku through exercises.

Migs Mayfeld, Burg, Qin, and Xi'an fear the worst during an attempted prison break.

Sibling Bond

Among Qin's rescuers is his twin sister, Xi'an. Qin would kill to protect his sister from others, but if the choice is between her life or his freedom Qin will always put his own needs first.

Quilted leather spats

QUEEN APAILANA

NABOO ROYALTY

DATA FILE

AFFILIATION: Republic
HOMEWORLD: Naboo
SPECIES: Human
HEIGHT: 1.57m (5ft 2in)
APPEARANCES: III
SEE ALSO: Padmé Amidala

Fan headdress worn in tribute to Padmé Amidala

THOUGH YOUNG, Queen Apailana has the qualities that the Naboo look for in their rulers: purity of heart and an absolute dedication to the peaceful values of the planet.

White makeup is ancient Naboo royal custom

Veda pearl suspensas

Cerlin capelet

QUEEN APAILANA is

elected Queen of Naboo when she is just 12 years old. One of the youngest monarchs in the planet's history, she begins her reign toward the end of the Clone Wars.

Chersilk mourning robe

Thousands follow Padmé Amidala's funeral procession through Theed.

Standing strong

Queen Apailana is one of the chief mourners at Padmé Amidala's funeral on Naboo. Padmé had supported Apailana's bid for election. Although the official explanation for Padmé's death is that she died at the hands of renegade Jedi, Apailana privately believes otherwise.

QUI-GON JINN

JEDI WHO DISCOVERS "THE CHOSEN ONE"

Qui-Gon Jinn is one of the few Jedi to have battled a Sith—Darth Maul.

Long hair worn back to keep vision clear

QUI-GON JINN
is an experienced but headstrong Jedi Master. He was Padawan to Count Dooku and teacher to Obi-Wan Kenobi. Jinn has sometimes clashed with the Jedi High Council over his favoring of risk and action: as a result, he has not been offered a seat on the Council.

Jedi tunic

Jinn's dying wish is that Obi-Wan trains Anakin.

The Chosen One

When Jinn encounters young Anakin Skywalker, he believes he has discovered the prophesized individual who will bring balance to the Force. Jinn makes a bet with Watto: if the boy wins his podrace, then he also wins his freedom. If he loses, Jinn loses his ship. The risk pays off, and Jinn takes the boy to Coruscant to present him to the Jedi High Council, with mixed results.

QUI-GON JINN
fights actively for the Galactic Republic, but he is struck down by the unruly dark energies of Darth Maul. After his death, Jinn becomes the first Jedi to live on in the Force, a gift he will pass on to Obi-Wan Kenobi, Yoda, and Anakin Skywalker.

Rugged travel boots

R2-D2

THE BRAVEST DROID IN THE GALAXY

DATA FILE

AFFILIATION: Republic; Rebel Alliance; Resistance
TYPE: Astromech droid
MANUFACTURER: Industrial Automaton
HEIGHT: 1.09m (3ft 7in)
APPEARANCES: I, II, III, RO, IV, V, VI, M, VII, VIII, IX
SEE ALSO: C-3PO; Luke Skywalker; Princess Leia

R2-D2 IS NO ORDINARY astromech droid. His long history of adventures has given him a distinct personality. He is stubborn and inventive, and is strongly motivated to succeed at any given task. Although R2-D2 speaks only in electronic beeps and whistles, he usually manages to make his point!

Holographic projector

R2-D2 has many hidden tricks, including extension arms and rocket boosters.

R2-D2 first distinguishes himself on board Queen Amidala's Royal Starship. He serves Anakin Skywalker during the Clone Wars and then Luke Skywalker during the Galactic Civil War, flying in the droid socket of their starfighters.

Powerbus cables

Motorized, all-terrain treads

Risky Mission

At the end of the Clone Wars, R2-D2 is assigned to Bail Organa's diplomatic fleet. Princess Leia entrusts R2-D2 with the stolen Death Star plans and her urgent message to Obi-Wan Kenobi. He risks all kinds of damage to accomplish his mission.

R4-P17

OBI-WAN KENOBI'S ASTROMECH DROID

DATA FILE

AFFILIATION: Republic
TYPE: Astromech droid
MANUFACTURER: Industrial
Automaton
HEIGHT: 96cm (3ft 2in)
APPEARANCES: II, III
SEE ALSO: Obi-Wan Kenobi

R4-P17 IS Obi-Wan Kenobi's trusty astromech droid, used in his red starfighter. Before the Clone Wars, she was copilot when Kenobi chased Jango Fett through the asteroid rings above Geonosis. R4-P17 continued to assist Obi-Wan during the Clone Wars and participated in the Battle of Teth among others.

R4-P17
compensates for Obi-Wan's dislike of flying by taking over most tasks, though he often asks her not to try any fancy maneuvers.

Onboard logic function displays

A buzz droid slices off R4-P17's domed head in the Battle of Coruscant.

Panels conceal tools

Standardized arm

Treaded drives

Repurposed
Before the Clone Wars, R4-P17 had a specially modified body, which fitted into the narrow wing of Kenobi's starfighter. She was later repurposed and now has a full astromech body so she can fit into the latest models of starfighters.

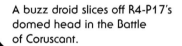

R5-D4

ASTROMECH DROID SET TO DESTRUCT

R5-D4, ALSO KNOWN as "Red," is a white-and-red astromech droid that Jawas on Tatooine sell to Owen Lars. However, immediately after the sale, Red's motivator blows up, and Owen returns him to the Jawas. This gives C-3PO the opportunity he needs to recommend that Owen purchase R2-D2 instead.

Photoreceptor

R5-D4 is eventually acquired by Peli Motto, who owns Hangar Bay 3-5 in Mos Eisley.

R5-D4 belongs to a series of droids that are cut-price versions of the superior R2 units. They are prone to defects and bad attitudes.

Panel conceals systems linkage and repair arms

Recharge coupling

Sabotage

What Owen and Luke do not know is that R2-D2 sabotaged R5-D4 when they were inside the Jawas' sandcrawler. Usually, droids' programming forbids them to mess with other droids, but Leia has instructed R2 to complete his mission at any cost.

Third tread for balance over uneven surfaces

RANZAR MALK

CRIMINAL CREW LEADER

DATA FILE

AFFILIATION: His own crew
HOMEWORLD Unknown
SPECIES: Human
HEIGHT: 1.73m (5ft 8in)
APPEARANCES: M
SEE ALSO: Burg; Migs
Mayfeld; Q9-0; Qin;
Xi'an

Malk and Qin celebrate double-crossing Din Djarin, unaware that the Mandalorian has alerted the New Republic to their location.

Leather flight jacket

Fingerless, insulated gloves sewn into jacket

RANZAR "RAN" Malk leads a group of mercenaries from a space station called the Roost. Malk appears happy to reunite with Din Djarin but hides important details from the Mandalorian about the mission.

Knee injured in previous job

EXPERIENCED Malk knows how to pull together crew members who will balance each other out and get a job done. No longer always at the front of the action, his bedraggled looks hide the still sharp and strategic mind of a scoundrel.

Complicated History

Malk, Din Djarin, and the Twi'lek siblings Xi'an and Qin have a history of running jobs together. Malk used to brag about having a Mandalorian on his team, but Din Djarin's abrupt departure left Malk and his crew reeling.

Spatter guards

RANGE TROOPER

DATA FILE

AFFILIATION: Empire
HOMEWORLD: Unknown
SPECIES: Human
HEIGHT (AVG.): 1.83m (6ft)
STANDARD EQUIPMENT:
E-10R blaster rifles
APPEARANCES: S
SEE ALSO: Stormtrooper

IN AN EXPANDING Empire, new territories are hard to control. As soldiers push their way onto new planets, it is the job of range troopers to maintain rule on these distant, and often hostile, worlds.

Controls for integrated gription boots

Rugged E-10R blaster rifle

RANGE TROOPERS

consider themselves the toughest of all the Imperial forces. These hard-core soldiers can withstand any environment. Their innate resilience is bolstered by extreme training, bespoke equipment, and ruthless determination to get the job done.

Kama lined with synth-fur

Heavy-duty magnatomic gription boots can adhere to high-speed trains.

Security Duty

On Vandor, the Empire stores coaxium hyperspace fuel. Range troopers must ensure that the conveyex transports run to schedule—and arrive with their cargo still on board.

RAPPERTUNIE

DATA FILE

AFFILIATION: Jabba's court
HOMEWORLD: Manpha
SPECIES: Shawda Ubb
HEIGHT: 30cm (1ft)
APPEARANCES: VI
SEE ALSO: Max Rebo

RAPPERTUNIE plays a combination flute, or Growdi Harmonique, in Max Rebo's Band. Rappertunie has always had a thirst for travel and has used his musical talent to pay his way around the galaxy. Unfortunately, he ends up in a lifetime gig at Jabba's palace, where the hot, dry climate does not suit his moist skin at all.

Defense

At Jabba's palace, Rappertunie can spend whole days perched motionless on his Growdi seat, trying to keep his naturally moist skin cool. Being small in size makes Rappertunie feel quite vulnerable, but he can spit paralyzing poison at those who threaten him.

RAPPERTUNIE

is a Shawda Ubb—a small, amphibious species with long fingers. Rappertunie was born on the swampy, wet Outer Rim planet Manpha.

Naturally moist skin

Three fingers adapted for amphibious life on home planet

Growdi

Rappertunie plays away at the rear of the stage while secretly plotting his escape.

RAZOO QIN-FEE

KANJIKLUB GANGSTER

A LIEUTENANT in the cutthroat Kanjiklub gang, Razoo Qin-Fee specializes in weapons maintenance and modification. The bandits of Kanjiklub favor crude and deadly weaponry and explosives. Qin-Fee upgrades and modifies them to dangerous specifications.

Homemade explosive cylinders

Spare blaster gas ammunition cartridge

AUTHORITY IN

Kanjiklub is a violent affair—as is everything in this Outer Rim gang. Razoo Qin-Fee eyes the role of leader, currently held by Tasu Leech. However, he must make enough allies first, so that he is not instantly overthrown by others in the gang.

Razoo Qin-Fee accompanies Tasu Leech while boarding Han Solo's freighter, the *Eravana*, in an ill-fated attempt to collect money that Solo owes Kanjiklub.

Lethal Lieutenant

Razoo Qin-Fee earned a dangerous reputation in the underworld Zygerrian fighting circuit, where he was banned for exceptionally dirty tactics. Though he is a fierce, unarmed warrior, he is also a pyromaniac and tech expert. His extensively modified blaster rifle, which he has named the "Wasp," packs a powerful sting.

REBEL TROOPER

GROUND FORCES OF THE REBEL ALLIANCE

DATA FILE

AFFILIATION: Rebel Alliance
HOMEWORLD: Various
SPECIES: Human
HEIGHT: Varies
STANDARD EQUIPMENT:
Blaster pistol
APPEARANCES: RO, IV, V, VI
SEE ALSO: General Madine

REBEL SOLDIERS are the main forces of the Alliance to Restore the Republic. These dedicated troops are organized into Sector Forces, each of which is responsible for resisting the might of the Empire in their home sectors across the galaxy.

A280-CFE
blaster rifle

Fleet troopers on the *Tantive IV* wear a uniform of blue shirts, black combat vests, and gray pants.

Cargo pants

REBEL TROOPS wear

standardized uniforms wherever the Alliance's meager resources allow. SpecForce wilderness fighters— soldiers trained for specialized roles in Alliance Special Forces— wear full forest-camouflaged fatigues during the Battle of Endor.

Commandos

Alliance SpecForce wilderness fighters infiltrate an Imperial base on Endor's forest moon. Under the command of General Solo, they manage to trick the squadrons of Imperial troops inside the base to come out, where they are outnumbered and forced to surrender.

Heavy-duty boots

REY

DATA FILE

AFFILIATION:
Resistance; Jedi;
Force Dyad
HOMEWORLD: Jakku
SPECIES: Human
HEIGHT: 1.7m (5ft 7in)
APPEARANCES: VII, VIII, IX
SEE ALSO: Ben Solo; Finn;
Kylo Ren; Luke Skywalker

Lightsaber
was Luke's
and, before
that, Anakin's

AT FIRST hesitant to leave her life as a scavenger on Jakku, Rey's strength in the Force, combined with her courage and compassion, helps her lead the Resistance to victory and inspires the best in those around her.

REY IS SURPRISED to learn that she has a vital role to play in the fate of the galaxy. She struggles to find her place in it all and is torn between the light and dark sides of the Force—and between Luke Skywalker and Kylo Ren.

Rey is the first person in many years to see Luke Skywalker when she tracks him down on the remote planet of Ahch-To.

First Order Refuser

Despite a hard life that should have left Rey free of sympathy and compassion, she looks for the best in people. She believes there is good in Kylo Ren and tries to reason with him. Together, they survive an encounter with Snoke and his Praetorian Guard, but Rey then refuses to join Ren when it becomes clear he is intent on a darker path than she is willing to follow.

Jakku gauze wraps combined with Jedi-style tunic

RIO DURANT

SPIRITED PILOT

DATA FILE

AFFILIATION: Tobias Beckett's crew; Crimson Dawn
HOMEWORLD: Ardennia
SPECIES: Ardennian
HEIGHT: 1.49m (4ft 11in)
APPEARANCES: S
SEE ALSO: Han Solo; Tobias Beckett; Val

Red-tinted flying goggles

Torplex LVD-41 pilot life-support kit

Rio tells a great story round the campfire, reliving crazy capers with all four of his arms.

AN ARDENNIAN pilot, Rio earned his wings with the Freedom Sons, fighting alongside the Republic in the Clone Wars. Now he uses his military skills in Tobias Beckett's criminal crew.

GENIAL RIO is good to have around in tense or dangerous situations. He lifts morale with jokes and stories. He is up for any scam, such as pretending to be choked by Beckett to clear a gaming table. He also loves to cook, which goes down well with teammates at the end of a long day.

Rio and Han

Rio is not sure about Han Solo joining the team at first, but he is won over in the end. He is glad to have Han with him when he is shot by a Cloud-Rider during the coaxium heist on Vandor. Rio's death makes a deep impression on Han and strengthens his resolve to find his long-lost love, Qi'ra.

Toes can grasp tools and controls

RIOT MAR

BOUNTY HUNTER AND PILOT

DATA FILE

AFFILIATION: Bounty Hunters Guild
HOMEWORLD: Unknown
SPECIES: Human
HEIGHT: 1.93m (6ft 4in)
APPEARANCES: M
SEE ALSO: Greef Karga; Grogu; the Mandalorian

RIOT MAR is an expert tracker who is a member of the Bounty Hunters Guild. He might show mercy if it helps him capture his prey, but he is hard to trust and might shoot the bounty if that makes things easier for him.

Blast shield with predatory teeth design

RIOT MAR is a top pilot and a great shot in his modified starfighter. He catches up to the Mandalorian near Tatooine. Mar offers to spare Grogu if Mando surrenders the child to him.

Target Practice

Riot Mar blasts and damages one of the engines of Mando's *Razor Crest*. Subsequently he believes the Mandalorian is trapped.

Life-support unit

Air-supply hose

Riot is outmaneuvered by the Mandalorian's superior piloting skills and firepower.

Pressurized g-suit

ROSE TICO

RESISTANCE COMMANDER

DATA FILE

AFFILIATION: Resistance
HOMEWORLD: Hays Minor
SPECIES: Human
HEIGHT: 1.57m (5ft 2in)
APPEARANCES: VIII, IX
SEE ALSO: DJ; Finn;
Paige Tico; Princess Leia

ROSE TICO doesn't let the death of her sister, Paige, keep her out of the fight to defeat the First Order. Rose works as a mechanic on the *Raddus*, joins Finn on a mission to Canto Bight, and fights with the Resistance at Exegol.

AFTER experiencing the brutality of the First Order on their home planet, Rose and her sister, Paige, joined the Resistance. It was Paige who gave Rose her sense of right and wrong and taught her to never give up. Rose's technical skills and logical mind prove very valuable to the Resistance.

Identification plaque

Mechanic's overalls

Coded override data spikes

Rose is starstruck to meet Finn, but she is equally capable when they go on a mission.

Electro-shock prod for stopping deserters

Problem Solver

Rose works her way up from an engineering support technician to a commander leading the Engineering Corps for the Resistance. Her kindness and devotion to her friends is noted by everyone, especially General Leia Organa.

RYSTÁLL SANT

PERFORMER IN THE MAX REBO BAND

DATA FILE

AFFILIATION: Jabba's court
HOMEWORLD: New Bornalex
SPECIES: Half Theelin/ half human
HEIGHT: 1.7m (5ft 7in)
APPEARANCES: III, VI
SEE ALSO: Oola

Natural markings highlighted with stage makeup

RYSTÁLL SANT'S adoptive parents are Ortolan musicians from Coruscant. They arrange for their dazzling daughter to perform as a singer and dancer with Max Rebo's band, where she will turn heads.

Rystáll and fellow singer Greeata are shocked by the depravities they witness at Jabba's palace.

RYSTÁLL IS part-human and part-Theelin. The Theelin are a rare species with head horns, brightly colored hair, and mottled skin. Rystáll also has hooved feet. Many Theelin are creative and choose to become artists or performers.

Cape is a gift from a passing admirer, Syrh Rhoams

Dancer's graceful body

Hooves

Star Attraction

Outgoing Rystáll Sant has always attracted the attention of a variety of characters, including the high-placed lieutenant in the criminal Black Sun organization, who enslaved her. Lando Calrissian later freed her. At Jabba's palace she attracts the attention of bounty hunter Boba Fett.

SABÉ

ROYAL NABOO HANDMAIDEN

DATA FILE

AFFILIATION: Royal House of Naboo
HOMEWORLD: Naboo
SPECIES: Human
HEIGHT: 1.65m (5ft 5in)
APPEARANCES: 1
SEE ALSO: Padmé Amidala

Royal headdress

Scar of remembrance

SABÉ IS THE MOST
important handmaiden in
Queen Amidala's entourage.
She is first in line to become
the royal decoy in times of
danger. Sabé dresses as the
queen and disguises her
features with white makeup.

Surcoat

Broad waistband

QUEEN AMIDALA'S
handmaidens assist with many
tasks necessary to maintain the
monarch's regal image. These
capable individuals are also
trained in bodyguard skills
and are equipped with
blaster pistols to defend their
monarch in the event of a
disturbance or emergency.

Long battle-dress made of blast-damping fabric

Sabé leads the delegation to
ask the Gungans to join the
Naboo in the fight for their planet.

Royal Service
While Sabé is disguised as the
queen, Padmé Amidala dresses
in the simple gown of a handmaiden.
They use silent gestures and expressions
to communicate secretly with each other.
Sabé is trained to imitate the queen in
every way, but the task is a risky one.

SAESEE TIIN

IKTOTCHI JEDI MASTER

DATA FILE

AFFILIATION: Jedi
HOMEWORLD: Iktotch
SPECIES: Iktotchi
HEIGHT: 1.88m (6ft 2in)
APPEARANCES: I, II, III
SEE ALSO: Mace Windu

JEDI MASTER SAESEE TIIN sits on the High Council in the Jedi Temple on Coruscant. He is particularly skilled in piloting the finest spacecraft at high speeds, which is also when his telepathic mind does its most focused thinking.

Well-developed horns

Lightsaber

Customary humanoid Jedi robes

Tough skin protects against high winds of Iktotchon

SAESEE TIIN was born on Iktotch, the moon of Iktotchon. He is a natural pilot, exhibiting an instinctive sense of direction and a fine control of ships of many different sizes. During an important Clone Wars mission to Lola Sayu, the site of the Separatist Citadel installation, Tiin pilots his well-maintained starfighter into battle.

Jedi Fighter

Saesee Tiin fights at the Battle of Geonosis, riding on a Republic gunship to attack the droids on the plains. Later in the battle, Tiin takes to the skies to aid Jedi Master Adi Gallia in the battle above Geonosis. Tiin becomes a general in the Clone Wars, leading starfighter squadrons.

Tiin is one of the Jedi who confront Palpatine, now revealed to be Sidious.

SALACIOUS B. CRUMB

KOWAKIAN MONKEY-LIZARD

DATA FILE

AFFILIATION: Jabba's court
HOMEWORLD: Kowak
SPECIES: Kowakian
monkey-lizard
HEIGHT: 70cm (2ft 4in)
APPEARANCES: VI
SEE ALSO: Jabba the Hutt

Highly
sensitive ears

SALACIOUS B. CRUMB is Jabba the Hutt's court jester. When Jabba first found this Kowakian monkey-lizard stealing his food, the Hutt tried to eat him. Crumb escaped but Bib Fortuna captured him.

Hooked reptilian beak

Collar of scruffy fur

Spindly arm

Crumb often irritates guests by repeating whatever Jabba says.

In Jest

Salacious B. Crumb knows that he must make Jabba laugh at least once a day, otherwise he will be killed. Crumb picks on everyone around him to entertain his boss, especially Jabba's new translator droid, C-3PO, who loses an eye to the hateful little creature.

SALACIOUS B. CRUMB

was just one of the many vermin on a space station, until he managed to stow away on board one of Jabba's spaceships, ending up on Tatooine. Now Crumb sits beside Jabba the Hutt, teasing all the inhabitants of the palace.

Sharp talons

SANDTROOPER

DESERT-READY STORMTROOPERS

DATA FILE

AFFILIATION: Empire
HOMEWORLD: Various
SPECIES: Human
HEIGHT (AVG.): 1.83m (6ft)
STANDARD EQUIPMENT:
Blaster pistol; blaster rifle;
repeating blaster
APPEARANCES: RO, IV
SEE ALSO: Stormtrooper

SANDTROOPERS ARE specialized Imperial stormtroopers, trained to adapt to desert environments. They are equipped with armor and weapons for use in hot, dry climates. Their armor uses advanced cooling systems, and their helmets have built-in polarized lenses to reduce sun glare.

SD-48 survival backpack

Pauldron indicates rank

Utility belt

Ranks

Sandtroopers wear shoulder pauldrons, which indicate rank. Regular sandtroopers' pauldrons are black, while sergeants wear white pauldrons. Squad leaders, who lead units of seven troopers, wear orange pauldrons.

SANDTROOPERS ARE

human recruits who remain anonymous behind their white armor. They carry food and water supplies, blaster rifles, and long-range comlinks. Sandtroopers' training enables them to adapt to local customs, such as riding native dewback lizards on Tatooine.

SARCO PLANK

GALACTIC OUTLAW

A SCAVENGER and bounty hunter, the sinister Sarco Plank works as an arms trader at Niima Outpost on Jakku, where he sells weapons to explorers willing to brave the desert wastes in search of valuable salvage.

Vocoder helmet

Nutrient and fluid dispenser

DURING THE Galactic Civil War, Sarco worked as a tomb raider, robbing ancient sites such as the Temple of Eedit, a Jedi outpost on Devaron. In that expedition, Sarco lured a young Luke Skywalker to the temple, hoping the youth could unlock the site's secrets. Sarco fought Luke, wielding an electrostaff against Skywalker's lightsaber, but failed to defeat the rebel pilot.

Eyeless Alien

Sarco Plank lacks eyes—his face is a featureless wall of insectoid plates. He senses his surroundings based on vibrations transmitted by ultra-sensitive hairs known as cilia, which line his body. A vocoder built into his feeding mask translates the humming of his face plates into an understandable voice.

SAW GERRERA

BATTLE-DAMAGED WARRIOR

AFFILIATION: Gerrera's Partisans
HOMEWORLD: Onderon
SPECIES: Human
HEIGHT: 1.8m (5ft 11in)
APPEARANCES: RO
SEE ALSO: Bodhi Rook; Jyn Erso

CONSIDERED TOO extreme even for the Rebel Alliance, Saw Gerrera sets up his own ragtag militia. His obsession to stop the Empire comes at any cost, often even endangering civilians.

YEARS OF fighting have left Saw's body damaged and weak. He wears a pressurized suit to help him breathe. What is left of his warrior's body is flooded with dangerous levels of medicine. It is dispensed to him by G2-1B7, a medical droid he has reprogrammed to bypass safety levels.

Breathing tube

Dxunwood walking stick

Old Onderonian banner worn as a cape

Gerrera raised Jyn from the age of eight, as part of his criminal cell.

Suspicious Gerrera

Gerrera's distrust has developed into paranoia in his old age. When an Imperial pilot defects to him, he cannot trust his motives. After using the tentacled Bor Gullet to read the pilot's mind—even at the possible cost of his sanity—Gerrera is still convinced that the pilot is a trap.

Cybernetic foot plate

SCOUT TROOPER

SPECIALIZED STORMTROOPERS

DATA FILE

AFFILIATION: Empire
HOMEWORLD: Various
SPECIES: Human
HEIGHT: Varies
STANDARD EQUIPMENT:
Blaster pistol; grenades;
survival gear
APPEARANCES: VI, M
SEE ALSO: Patrol Trooper;
Sandtrooper; Stormtrooper

Visor enhances vision

IMPERIAL SCOUT TROOPERS

are trained for long-term missions.
They wear armor on their head
and upper body only, to allow
maximum maneuverability.
Their helmets have
enhanced macrobinocular
viewplates, for precision
target identification.

Body glove

IMPERIAL SCOUT

troopers are
sent to survey areas and
locate enemy positions,
infiltrate enemy territory,
and undertake sabotage
missions. They rarely engage
in combat, and are instructed
to call in stormtroopers at any
signs of trouble.

The Republic first deployed
clone scout troopers during the
Clone Wars, including at the
Battle of Kachirho on Kashyyyk.

Durable boot

On Patrol

Scout troopers on speeder bikes
patrol the dense forests of Endor,
where the Empire maintains a
strategic shield generator. Working
in units of two or four, they watch
for any signs of troublesome forest
creatures or terrorist infiltrators.

SEBULBA

STAR PODRACER

DATA FILE

AFFILIATION: None
HOMEWORLD: Malastare
SPECIES: Dug
HEIGHT: 1.12m (3ft 8in)
APPEARANCES: I
SEE ALSO: Anakin Skywalker

SEBULBA IS ONE of the top podracers in the Outer Rim circuits. He is skilled at piloting his vehicle, but also willing to use dirty tricks to give him the winning edge. When Anakin Skywalker joins a race, Sebulba decides the young human must not win.

Grasping hands

Race goggles

Beaded danglers

SEBULBA
is a Dug from Malastare, a species notorious for being bullies. Playing up to his tough, violent image for the crowds, Sebulba wears a flashy, custom-designed leather racing suit.

Leather wrist guard

Sebulba pilots a giant orange podracer with many secret weapons concealed in it.

Trophy coins

Although Sebulba crashes during the Boonta Eve Classic, he survives to race in other competitions.

Dangerous Driver
The dastardly Dug gives himself the winning edge in races by sabotaging other racers. Sebulba can pull up alongside another podracer and blast it with his hidden flamethrower, or throw concussion weapons into another pilot's cockpit.

Tight leather leg-straps

SHAAK TI

TOGRUTA JEDI MASTER

DATA FILE

AFFILIATION: Jedi
HOMEWORLD: Shili
SPECIES: Togruta
HEIGHT: 1.78m (5ft 10in)
APPEARANCES: II, III
SEE ALSO: Luminara Unduli

Characteristic pigmentation of the Togruta species

Two-handed grip for control

Jedi robe

JEDI MASTER SHAAK TI joined the Jedi High Council before the Battle of Geonosis. During the Clone Wars, she often represents the Jedi Order on Kamino. Her compassion for the clone troopers as individuals clashes with the Kaminoan scientists' cold view that they are products.

Hollow montrals sense space

Shaak Ti is the same species as Anakin Skywalker's apprentice, Ahsoka Tano.

Master Jedi

Shaak Ti fights alongside more than 200 other Jedi Knights that come to the aid of Anakin Skywalker, Obi-Wan Kenobi, and Padmé Amidala on Geonosis. After the conflict in the arena, she boards a Republic gunship for the front lines of the battle against the massed droid army.

TOGRUTA Shaak Ti is one of the best Jedi fighters in group combat. Her hollow head montrals sense space ultrasonically, sharpening her spatial awareness. Where others struggle with the complexity of movements, Shaak Ti darts with ease.

SHMI SKYWALKER

ANAKIN SKYWALKER'S MOTHER

DATA FILE

AFFILIATION: None
HOMEWORLD: Tatooine
SPECIES: Human
HEIGHT: 1.73m (5ft 8in)
APPEARANCES: I, II
SEE ALSO: Anakin Skywalker;
Cliegg Lars; Tusken Raider;
Watto

SHMI SKYWALKER HAS lived a hard life since pirates captured her parents when she was a girl, but she remains brave and resourceful. While enslaved to junk dealer Watto on Tatooine, Shmi gives birth to a child named Anakin.

Decorative belt

IN SPITE OF her poverty, Shmi tries to give Anakin a good home in Mos Espa. Anakin's departure is hard for Shmi to bear, but she comes to live a happier life when a settler farmer, Cliegg Lars, frees her in order to marry her.

Rough-spun tunic withstands harsh Tatooine weather

Tragic Loss

When Anakin Skywalker senses that his mother is in anguish, he travels to Tatooine to help her. However, he cannot prevent her death at the hands of the Sand People. Experiencing great anger and pain, Anakin vows to build his power until nothing can withstand it

Shmi refuses to let her love for Anakin keep him from what she feels is his destiny—to be a Jedi.

Simple skirt

SHOCK TROOPER

MEMBERS OF THE CORUSCANT GUARD

DATA FILE

AFFILIATION: Republic; Empire
HOMEWORLD: Kamino
SPECIES: Human (clone)
HEIGHT: 1.83m (6ft)
STANDARD EQUIPMENT: DC-15 blaster rifle
APPEARANCES: II, III
SEE ALSO: Stormtrooper

AS THE REPUBLIC PREPARES for war, red-emblazoned shock troopers begin to patrol public spaces on Coruscant, to ensure public order and security. They also serve as bodyguards for politicians, including Supreme Chancellor Palpatine.

Upgraded breath filter and annunciator

Coruscant designation

Shock-absorbing plastoid armor

DC-15 blaster rifle

In the last days of the Republic, people begin to refer to shock troopers as stormtroopers.

SHOCK TROOPERS

are members of the Coruscant Guard. Palpatine set up the unit to strengthen the Coruscant Security Force and the Senate Guard. Shock troopers keep watch on government buildings and landing platforms.

Palpatine's Guard

Shock troopers go with Palpatine to the Senate after the Jedi's failed attempt to arrest him. Following Yoda's battle with Palpatine, they unsuccessfully search for the Jedi Master's body. Shock troopers also accompany Palpatine to Mustafar, where they find Vader burned.

SHORETROOPER

BEACH STORMTROOPERS

DATA FILE

AFFILIATION: Empire
HOMEWORLD: Various
SPECIES: Human
HEIGHT (AVG.): 1.83m (6ft)
STANDARD EQUIPMENT:
E-22 blaster rifle
APPEARANCES: RO, M
SEE ALSO: Stormtrooper

Air filter

SHORETROOPERS stand out against the plain white armor of regular stormtroopers, but blend in with sand and palm tree trunks. They are specially trained and equipped for coastal environments such as Scarif, which houses the high-security Citadel complex. They are also present at the Morak rhydonium refining facility, operated by the Imperial Remnant.

Belt contains ammunition for blaster weapons

MOST shoretroopers are sergeants, so would have operational command over regular stormtroopers. However, Scarif is such a fortified planet that few people expect an attack to ever come close to the Citadel.

Shoretroopers are ready to face the unexpected, such as rebels inside the perimeter.

Leg armor expands

Beach Ready

Shoretroopers are equipped for their environment. Fans in their helmets keep them cool and air filters reduce sand inhalation. Temperature-controlled bodysuits are sealed under lightweight armor, which has a special coating to prevent salt damage from the sea air.

SHU MAI

PRESIDENT OF THE COMMERCE GUILD

DATA FILE

AFFILIATION: Commerce Guild; Separatists
HOMEWORLD: Castell
SPECIES: Gossam
HEIGHT: 1.65m (5ft 5in)
APPEARANCES: II, III
SEE ALSO: Count Dooku; Nute Gunray; Wat Tambor

Shu Mai awaits her fate on volcanic Mustafar with the rest of the Separatist leaders.

Neck rings

Emblazoned jewel crest

SHU MAI IS PRESIDENT of the powerful Commerce Guild, whose forces fight the Republic during the Clone Wars. Mai is a member of the Separatist Council alongside Nute Gunray, Wat Tambor, and others.

Rich skirt made of rare uris silk

SHU MAI is a Gossam from the planet Castell. She is only concerned with status, power, and wealth. Mai worked her way up the Commerce Guild using aggressive and unscrupulous tactics, until no rivals stood in her way to becoming president.

Gossams have three-toed feet

Sneaky Practices

Shu Mai is not the only Separatist leader to pledge her support to Dooku in secret, knowing that it amounts to treason. Though the Commerce Guild does not openly back the Separatists, Shu Mai's homing spider droids begin to fight on the battlefields of the Clone Wars.

SIO BIBBLE

GOVERNOR OF NABOO

DATA FILE

AFFILIATION: Royal House of Naboo
HOMEWORLD: Naboo
SPECIES: Human
HEIGHT: 1.7m (5ft 7in)
APPEARANCES: I, II, III
SEE ALSO: Captain Panaka; Nute Gunray; Padmé Amidala

Formal collar

SIO BIBBLE is Governor of Naboo during the Trade Federation invasion. He oversees all matters brought to Queen Amidala's attention. He also chairs the Advisory Council, the governing body of Naboo. Sio is completely opposed to violence.

Fashionable Naboo sleeves and cuffs

Philosopher's tunic

BIBBLE IS A

philosopher who was elected governor under Amidala's predecessor. Sio is initially critical of Amidala, but comes to respect her. He later serves under a number of Amidala's successors, including Queens Jamillia, Neeyutnee, and Apailana.

Bibble refuses to accept Captain Panaka's warnings of greater need for armament.

Under Arrest

During the invasion of Naboo, battle droids arrest Sio Bibble and Queen Amidala. When two Jedi Knights rescue Amidala, the governor chooses to stay with his people. Bibble leads them in a hunger strike and earns the ire of the Trade Federation Viceroy, Nute Gunray.

Governor's boots

SITH CULTIST

DARK-SIDE FANATICS

DATA FILE

AFFILIATION: Acolytes of the Beyond; Alazmec of Winsit; Sith Eternal
HOMEWORLD: Exegol
SPECIES: Unknown
HEIGHT: Varies
APPEARANCES: IX
SEE ALSO: Alazmec Colonist; Ochi of Bestoon; Palpatine

Laboratory gloves

Hood length indicates years of service to the Sith

Face coverings

Palpatine's death produces a flash of dark-side energy that destroys the Sith Citadel and its cultists.

SITH CULTISTS devote their lives to worshipping and protecting the legacy of the Sith. To this end, they help Palpatine cheat death with cloning technology and build a huge fleet of new-generation Star Destroyers.

SITH ETERNAL

cultists are just one of many Sith cults. The Acolytes of the Beyond dedicate themselves to attacking the New Republic, while the Alazmec of Winsit cultists preserve the ruins of Vader's castle on Mustafar.

Oversize robe hides cultist's identity

Sith Citadel

On Exegol, Sith Eternal cultists inhabit a Sith Citadel, where they protect the unstable clone of their master, Palpatine. In the Citadel's dark-science laboratory, Palpatine created Snoke.

SITH JET TROOPER

AERIAL ASSAULT SITH TROOPERS

DATA FILE

AFFILIATION: Sith Eternal; Final Order
HOMEWORLD: Exegol
SPECIES: Human
HEIGHT: Varies
STANDARD EQUIPMENT: Heavy cannon; jetpack
APPEARANCES: IX
SEE ALSO: Sith Trooper; Sovereign Protector

Airtight helmet

A jet trooper spins out of control after being hit by an arrow fired by Resistance ally Jannah.

NJP-900 jetpack

Multi-layered armor

F-11ABA heavy cannon

SITH JET TROOPERS are elite soldiers trained for high-altitude air combat. They are employed in battle during rapid air strikes and as air cover when Sith troopers are attacking combatants on the ground.

Sealed body glove

SITH JET TROOPER squad names, such as Lanvorak Squad, Parange Squad, and Warblade Squad, honor the names of ancient, highly destructive dark-side weapons.

Taking Flight

Jet trooper jetpacks can run on jet mode or rocket mode. Rocket mode uses more fuel but is more reliable in thin or zero atmosphere environments.

SITH TROOPER

FINAL ORDER STORMTROOPERS

DATA FILE

AFFILIATION: Sith Eternal; Final Order
HOMEWORLD: Exegol
SPECIES: Human
HEIGHT: Varies
STANDARD EQUIPMENT: ST-W48 blaster rifles; SONN-BLAS FWMB-10B repeating blasters
APPEARANCES: IX
SEE ALSO: Sith Jet Trooper; Sovereign Protector

Enhanced visibility visor

A squad of Sith troopers consists of 10 soldiers. Three-trooper fire teams are referred to as triads.

Impact-resistant armor

ST-W48 blaster

SITH TROOPERS ARE elite stormtroopers trained for Palpatine's secret Sith Eternal army on Exegol. Sith troopers wear red armor as an intimidating sign of their loyalty to the dark side.

Red armor evokes aura of dread

SITH TROOPERS are not sensitive to the Force and, like First Order troopers, are not clones. However, they are specially trained to suppress all their individuality and become absolutely loyal to Palpatine.

Into Battle

Sith troopers are deployed at the Battle of Exegol. Yet even these elite troops are unprepared for Resistance fighters that ride equine-like orbaks onto the hull of the First Order Star Destroyer the *Steadfast*.

SLY MOORE

PALPATINE'S STAFF AIDE

Eyes see only in ultraviolet light

SLY MOORE is Palpatine's staff aide. She wields huge power because she controls access to the Chancellor. Moore is one of the few individuals who knows that Palpatine's secret identity is Darth Sidious. She continues to serve him when he becomes Emperor.

Sly Moore often attends Palpatine's meetings, silently shadowing the Supreme Chancellor.

SLY MOORE is an Umbaran—a technologically advanced species from Umbara. This planet is known as "the Shadow World" because so little natural light reaches its surface. Umbarans are known for their ability to use their minds to subtly influence, and control, others.

Power Play

In Palpatine's administration, Sly Moore holds the post that Sei Taria had in Chancellor Valorum's time. Some whisper that Moore must have threatened the committed and dedicated Sei Taria with blackmail to persuade her to stand down.

Umbaran shadow cloak is patterned in ultraviolet colors

SNAP WEXLEY

RESISTANCE RECON PILOT

DATA FILE

AFFILIATION: Resistance
HOMEWORLD: Akiva
SPECIES: Human
HEIGHT: 1.88m (6ft 2in)
APPEARANCES: VII, IX
SEE ALSO: Jess Pava; Poe Dameron; Princess Leia

A SKILLED X-wing pilot serving in Blue Squadron, Temmin "Snap" Wexley is a captain in the Resistance, and recognized by Poe Dameron as the best recon flier in the force.

FreiTek life-support unit

Inflatable life vest

Flight helmet

Snap's last flight is at the Battle of Exegol where he dies fighting the Final Order fleet.

Rebel Roots

The son of Norra Wexley, a veteran Y-wing pilot who flew at the Battle of Endor, Snap hails from Akiva, an Outer Rim world that was an Imperial base prior to its liberation by the New Republic. At that time, young Wexley learned street-smarts and survived with the help of his protector, a modified battle droid named Mister Bones.

AFTER THE STARKILLER

weapon destroys the New Republic's capital world, Resistance controllers are able to triangulate its location. Snap Wexley flies a daring recon mission into the Unknown Regions, and records vital information about the secret base that allows the Resistance to formulate an attack strategy.

SNOWTROOPER

EXTREME-CLIMATE STORMTROOPERS

Polarized snow goggles

DATA FILE

AFFILIATION: Empire
HOMEWORLD: Various
SPECIES: Human
HEIGHT (AVG.): 1.83m (6ft)
STANDARD EQUIPMENT: E-11
blaster rifle; light repeating
blasters; grenades
APPEARANCES: V
SEE ALSO: Shock trooper

IMPERIAL SNOWTROOPERS

are specialized stormtroopers that
form self-sufficient mobile combat
units in environments of snow
and ice. Their backpacks
and suit systems keep
their bodies warm,
while their face masks
are equipped with
breath heaters.

E-11 blaster rifle

THE EMPIRE modeled its
snowtroopers on the Galactic
Republic's specialized clone cold
assault troopers, who fought
in the Clone Wars on frozen
worlds such as Orto Plutonia.

Storage pouch

Insulated belt cape

Snowtroopers carry and set up
deadly E-web heavy repeating
blasters in snowy terrain.

Rugged ice boots

Assault on Hoth

Snowtroopers are deployed as part of
General Veers' Blizzard Force at the
Battle of Hoth. Snowtroopers work in
tandem with AT-AT walkers to affect a
massive strike. They defeat the forces
of the Rebel Alliance and break into Echo
Base. These specialized soldiers can
survive for two weeks in extreme cold
terrain on suit battery power alone.

SOVEREIGN PROTECTOR

PALPATINE'S BODYGUARDS

DATA FILE

AFFILIATION: Sith Eternal
HOMEWORLD: Exegol
SPECIES: Unknown
HEIGHT: Varies
STANDARD EQUIPMENT:
SP-B50 blaster rifle with vibro-active force blade
APPEARANCES: IX
SEE ALSO: Sith trooper

Modified Sith Helmet

Sovereign Protectors always try to circle their prey to limit their movements.

SP-B50 blaster rifle

THE SOVEREIGN

Protectors are the most ruthless, fanatical, and loyal soldiers ever trained by the Sith Eternal. They are stationed in the Sith Citadel on Exegol to protect the weakened Palpatine from external threats.

Final Stand

On Exegol, Rey is met by Sovereign Protectors who are all that stand between her and Palpatine. She uses her immense Force powers to redirect their blaster fire back at each other.

LIKE SITH ETERNAL

officers, many Sovereign Protectors are the children of Sith Cultists, born and raised on Exegol. To protect their methods, all training for Sovereign Protectors is done in secrecy.

High-traction boots

STASS ALLIE

THOLOTHIAN JEDI MASTER

Tholoth tendrils

Common lightsaber design

THOLOTHIAN JEDI MASTER

Stass Allie serves the Republic during the Clone Wars. As the cousin of a highly distinguished Jedi, Adi Gallia, Allie is keen to demonstrate her own abilities. After Gallia's death in the Clone Wars, Allie takes her place on the Jedi Council.

Utility belt

Stass Allie patrols Saleucami on a speeder bike, where she will lose her life to Order 66.

STASS ALLIE is a formidable warrior, but her talent for battlefield medicine is also impressive. These first-aid skills have saved the lives of troops under her command during the Clone Wars.

Brave Fighter

Joining Mace Windu's Jedi task force to Geonosis, Stass Allie participates in the arena battle. She is one of the few survivors, continuing to fight as the battle escalates outside the arena.

Tall travel boots

STORMTROOPER

THE EMPIRE'S ELITE SOLDIERS

DATA FILE

AFFILIATION: Empire
HOMEWORLD: Various
SPECIES: Human
HEIGHT (AVG.): 1.83m (6ft)
STANDARD EQUIPMENT:
E-11 blaster rifle; thermal detonator
APPEARANCES: S, RO, IV, V, VI, M
SEE ALSO: Snowtrooper

STORMTROOPERS MAKE UP the bulk of the Imperial military's armed forces, and are feared by inhabitants across a thousand worlds. They are highly disciplined and completely loyal to the Emperor, carrying out commands without hesitation.

Blaster power cell container

STORMTROOPERS

are human recruits who remain anonymous behind their white armor, which protects them from harsh environments and glancing shots from blaster bolts.

Reinforced alloy plate ridge

The massed ranks of armored stormtroopers obey their orders unquestioningly.

Sniper position knee protector plate

Fight to Win

In battle, stormtroopers are trained to ignore casualties within their own ranks. Notice is only taken from a tactical standpoint. Stormtroopers are never distracted by emotional responses.

Positive-grip boots

SUPER BATTLE DROID

UPGRADED BATTLE DROID

DATA FILE

AFFILIATION: Separatists
TYPE: B2 super battle droid
MANUFACTURER: Baktoid
Combat Automata
HEIGHT: 1.93m (6ft 4in)
APPEARANCES: II, III, M
SEE ALSO: Battle droid

Arms stronger
than battle
droid limbs

Monogrip
hands are hard
to damage

AFTER THE TRADE FEDERATION'S
defeat in the Battle of Naboo, its leaders
commissioned an improved battle droid.
Tough and heavily armed, super
battle droids break Republic
regulations on private security
forces. However, the Neimoidians
have too much influence to care.

THE DROID

foundries of Geonosis
secretly manufacture
super battle droids.
They have standard
battle droid internal
components for
economy, but
they utilize a much
stronger shell.

Flexible
armored
midsection

Excess
heat radiated
through calf vanes

Fearless Droids

Super battle droids can be poor at
formulating attack plans. However,
they make up for this lack by their
fearlessness in battle, reducing
their targets to ruins.

Strap-on foot tips
can be replaced
with claws or pads

R2-D2 has his own way of fighting
super battle droids: he shoots oil
at them, before setting them on fire.

SUPREME LEADER SNOKE

ARCHITECT OF THE FIRST ORDER

Scar channel

DATA FILE

AFFILIATION: First Order
HOMEWORLD: Exegol
SPECIES: Genetic strandcast
HEIGHT: More than 2.1m
(6ft 11in)
APPEARANCES: VII, VIII
SEE ALSO: General Hux;
Kylo Ren; Palpatine
Praetorian Guard

Sunken face caused
by malformed bone

LIFE UNDER Supreme Leader Snoke's First Order is cruel and terrifying. The dictator's every whim is enforced without question by a high-tech, well-trained army of stormtroopers.

On Exegol, Kylo Ren learns that Snoke was created by Palpatine and used by the Emperor to manipulate him and the First Order.

Master of Manipulation

Snoke understands the power of fear and reputation, so he is rarely seen in person. Instead, he gives orders via hologram. His enlarged, grotesque image comes across as even more monstrous than he is in the flesh.

ALTHOUGH HE IS NOT a Sith, Snoke has many Force abilities. He has mastered telepathy, mind probing, telekinesis, choke, and lightning attacks. Following ancient Sith traditions, he also takes an apprentice, Kylo Ren. Snoke exploits Ren's weaknesses so that he will do the Supreme Leader's bidding for him.

Extravagant
gold-flecked robes

SY SNOOTLES

LEAD VOCALIST FOR THE MAX REBO BAND

DATA FILE

AFFILIATION: Jabba's court
HOMEWORLD: Lowick
SPECIES: Pa'lowick
HEIGHT: 1.6m (5ft 3in)
APPEARANCES: VI
SEE ALSO: Jabba the Hutt;
Max Rebo

Expressive mouth

Retractable tusks protrude from second mouth

Powerful chest for swimming— and singing!

Pa'lowicks have lean limbs, round bodies, eye-stalks, and long lip-stalks.

Skin coloration provides camouflage in swamps of homeworld

SY SNOOTLES IS A

Pa'lowick singer and lead vocalist for the Max Rebo Band when they played at Jabba's palace. Snootles only agrees to join the band on the strict condition that Rebo also hires her good friend, Greeata Jendowanian, as a dancer and singer.

Microphone stand

Forward and backward-facing toes for walking on shallow lakes

SNOOTLES has had an adventurous life. She used to be Ziro the Hutt's lover but then, on discovering the true extent of his cruelty, became his assassin. In Jabba's palace, Snootles works as a double agent, feeding Bib Fortuna's lies to Jabba's enemies.

Strange Singing

Jabba's appreciation of Sy Snootles' singing has given her a vastly inflated idea of her own talent. When the band splits up after Jabba's death, Snootles finds it hard to make it anywhere mainstream—the chief reason being her vocals are just too weird.

TALLISSAN "TALLIE" LINTRA

BLUE LEADER AT D'QAR

DATA FILE

AFFILIATION: Resistance; Blue Squadron
HOMEWORLD: Pippip 3
SPECIES: Human
HEIGHT: 1.73m (5ft 8in)
APPEARANCES: VIII
SEE ALSO: Paige Tico; Poe Dameron

TALLIE LINTRA'S flying career began with spraying crops on her parents' farm in a RZ-1 A-wing adapted into a cropduster. Now she flies a RZ-2 A-wing for the Resistance and is one of their finest pilots.

Synthsilk scarf was a gift from her father

Standard-issue green flight suit

TALLIE proves herself to be a highly capable pilot, impressing even Poe Dameron with her skills. Her role in the Resistance is varied. She flies relief missions, defends larger craft, attacks targets, and engages in dogfights with First Order TIE fighters.

Blue One

During the Evacuation of D'Qar, Squadron Leader Lintra flies as Blue One, leading Blue Squadron. The starfighters escort and cover the MG-100 StarFortress bombers that contain enough firepower to bring down the *Fulminatrix*—the First Order Dreadnought.

Guidenhauser ejection harness

Tallie is revved up and about to take off from the *Raddus'* hangar when it is hit by shots from Kylo Ren's TIE silencer.

TANK TROOPER

IMPERIAL PATROLLERS

DATA FILE

AFFILIATION: Empire
HOMEWORLD: Various
SPECIES: Human
HEIGHT (AVG.): 1.83m (6ft)
STANDARD VEHICLE:
TX-225 "Occupier" combat
assault tank
APPEARANCES: RO, M
SEE ALSO: AT-AT pilot

TANK TROOPERS are stormtroopers trained for Imperial ground assault vehicles. One assignment could be ferrying troops in huge transports. The next could be leading an assault in a heavily armed tank.

Air filter

Lightweight armor for squeezing in a tank

Tanks carry looted kyber crystals out of Jedha City so they can be sent offworld.

A TRIO of terror, tank troopers work in teams of three: a driver, a gunner, and a tank commander on top. The driver is also responsible for the tank's maintenance.

Sitting Ducks

Bulky TX-225 tanks are a strong statement of power, but they also make troopers an easy target for rebellious locals. And there is no quick way out of Jedha's winding streets.

TARFFUL

WOOKIEE CHIEFTAIN

DATA FILE

AFFILIATION: Republic
HOMEWORLD: Kashyyyk
SPECIES: Wookiee
HEIGHT: 2.34m (7ft 8in)
APPEARANCES: III
SEE ALSO: Chewbacca

Teeth bared
for war cry

TARFFUL IS LEADER of the Wookiee city of Kachirho. When the Separatist forces invade his planet, Kashyyyk, Tarfful works with Chewbacca and Jedi Yoda, Luminara Unduli, and Quinlan Vos to plan the Wookiees' strategy for repelling the invaders.

Decorative
pauldron

Orb-igniter

Tarfful and Chewbacca help Yoda flee in a hidden escape pod after Order 66.

TARFFUL WAS

once enslaved by the Trandoshan slavers, who have long been the enemies of the Wookiees. When clone troops rescued him, Tarfful pledged to fight anyone who tried to enslave his people or capture his planet.

Thick calf
muscles from
climbing trees

Fur protects
upper foot

Wookiee Attack

Tarfful is a calm, considerate Wookiee who can be a mighty warrior when necessary. He leads his fellow Wookiees in daring raids on amphibious Separatist tank droids.

TASU LEECH

KANJIKLUB LEADER

DATA FILE

AFFILIATION: Kanjiklub
HOMEWORLD: Nar Kanji
SPECIES: Human
HEIGHT: 1.57m (5ft 2in)
APPEARANCES: VII
SEE ALSO: Chewbacca;
Han Solo; Kanjiklub gang;
Razoo Qin-Fee

TASU LEECH IS the current leader of the notorious Kanjiklub gang. He is an unruly street fighter who firmly holds onto his position by showing no signs of weakness.

Plastoid blast jerkin

Spare ammunition

TASU LEECH

grew up on Nar Kanji, on the frontiers of the galaxy, and clawed his way to the top of the Kanjiklub. He refuses to speak Basic, considering it a weak language of cowardly people.

"Huttsplitter" blaster rifle

Deal Gone Bad

Solo has twice before failed to deliver cargo to Kanjiklub, shortening Tasu's already violent temper. Boarding Solo's freighter in search of compensation, Tasu's standoff with Solo turns deadly when a shipment of rathtars escape, sending Kanjiklubbers scurrying for their lives.

TEEBO

EWOK MYSTIC

DATA FILE

AFFILIATION: Bright Tree Village
HOMEWORLD: Forest Moon of Endor
SPECIES: Ewok
HEIGHT: 1.24m (4ft 1in)
APPEARANCES: VI
SEE ALSO: Chief Chirpa; Logray

Churi feathers

Gurreck skull headdress

Teebo joins the Rebel Alliance with his fellow Ewoks to defeat the Imperial army on Endor.

Striped pelt

Authority stick

THE EWOK NAMED

Teebo is a watcher of the stars and a poet, and he has a mystical connection to the forces of nature. His keen perceptive abilities and practical thinking have made Teebo a leading figure within his tribe.

TEEBO had many adventures growing up in his tribe before becoming an apprentice of the tribal shaman, Logray. He is learning the ways of Ewok magic and hopes to become the tribe's shaman someday.

Aggressive Beginnings

When Teebo first sees Han Solo and his team, he distrusts them. After being freed from his bonds, R2-D2 promptly zaps Teebo's backside!

TEEDO

DATA FILE

AFFILIATION: None
HOMEWORLD: Jakku
SPECIES: Teedo
HEIGHT: 1.24m (4ft 1in)
APPEARANCES: VII
SEE ALSO: BB-8; Rey

TEEDOS ARE SMALL, brutish scavengers who roam the Jakku wilderness, often riding atop cyborg luggabeasts. They scour the dunes for salvageable technology and fiercely protect their findings with a tyrannical zeal.

Goggles

Mag-pulse grenade

Catch bottle recycles bodily fluids

TEEDOS HAVE a peculiar sense of individual identity—the name Teedo seems to identify both the species as a whole and each member within it. Despite their small size, Teedos have an exaggerated sense of their ability to intimidate.

Stealing BB-8

During BB-8's wanderings past Kelvin Ravine in the Jakku wastelands, the droid is snagged in a net by a luggabeast-riding Teedo. A young human scavenger, Rey, shouts down the surly Teedo, convincing the exasperated alien to give up his quarry after he deems the little droid not worth the hassle.

Scaly skin

Sand-shoes cut from droid treads

TESSEK

JABBA'S QUARREN ACCOUNTANT

Hearing organs

DATA FILE

AFFILIATION: Jabba's court
HOMEWORLD: Mon Cala
SPECIES: Quarren
HEIGHT: 1.8m (5ft 11in)
APPEARANCES: VI
SEE ALSO: Jabba the Hutt

Manipulative mouth tentacles

TESSEK IS EMPLOYED at Jabba's palace as the Hutt's accountant. But his loyalty to Jabba is a smokescreen. Behind the crime lord's back, Tessek plots to assassinate him and take over his criminal empire. But Tessek does not realize that Jabba probably knows this, too.

TESSEK is a Quarren from Mon Cala. He was involved in galactic politics until the Empire began to enslave his people. This caused Tessek to go into hiding on Tatooine, where he found use for his financial skills among the Hutt gangsters.

Scheming Reputation

Tessek lives up to some of the worst qualities attributed to the Quarren by outsiders. Because of the recurrent civil wars between them and the Mon Calamari, the Quarren have gained the reputation of being untrustworthy schemers willing to take any advantage.

Moisture-retaining robe

TIE FIGHTER PILOT

DATA FILE

AFFILIATION: Empire
HOMEWORLD: Various
SPECIES: Human
HEIGHT: Varies
STANDARD VEHICLE:
TIE-series starfighters
APPEARANCES: S, RO, IV,
V, VI, M
SEE ALSO: AT-AT pilot

Reinforced
flight helmet

Gas transfer hose

Life-support pack

TIE targeting systems and flight
controls are superior to anything
available to rebel starfighters.

TIE FIGHTER PILOTS

form an elite group
within the Imperial Navy.
These black-suited pilots are
conditioned to be entirely
dedicated to the mission and
to destroy their targets, even if
this causes their own deaths.

Vacuum g-suit

Energy-shielded fabric

FIGHTER PILOTS take
great pride in their TIE fighters, even
though the ships lack deflector shields
and hyperdrives. The product of
intense training at the Imperial
Academies, TIE pilots are taught they
are the best in the galaxy. As a result,
they are often quite arrogant.

Battle Ready

The Empire keeps TIE fighter pilots on a
constant state of alert so they are ready
for battle at any time. Each pilot wears
reinforced flight helmets, with breather
tubes connected to a life-support pack,
in case their TIE's cockpit is breached
on a mission.

TION MEDON

PORT ADMINISTRATOR OF PAU CITY

DATA FILE

AFFILIATION: Republic
HOMEWORLD: Utapau
SPECIES: Pau'an
HEIGHT: 2.06m (6ft 10in)
APPEARANCES: III
SEE ALSO: MagnaGuard;
Obi-Wan Kenobi

Gray, furrowed
skin from lack
of light in
sinkholes

Wide belt
supports
bony frame

Port master's
walking stick

TION MEDON
is a descendent of
Timon Medon, who
unified Utapau. Like
all Pau'ans, Tion
prefers darkness to
sunlight and raw
meat to cooked.

Floor-length
robes are a
recent fashion

Utapau's surface is windswept
and barren. The Utai and
Pau'ans live in cities within
huge sinkholes.

TION MEDON IS master
of Port Administration
for Pau City on Utapau.
MagnaGuards kill his committee
members, and the Separatist
leadership use his world as
a temporary sanctuary.

Under Pressure

When Jedi Obi-Wan Kenobi lands
at Pau City on Utapau, Tion Medon
reassures the Jedi that nothing strange
has happened. While Kenobi's ship is
refueled, Tion whispers that Separatists
have taken control of Utapau.

TOBIAS BECKETT

PROFESSIONAL THIEF

DATA FILE

AFFILIATION: His own crew; Crimson Dawn
HOMEWORLD: Glee Anselm
SPECIES: Human
HEIGHT: 1.78m (5ft 10in)
APPEARANCES: S
SEE ALSO: Han Solo; Rio Durant; Val

TOBIAS BECKETT is always scheming. He works with his crew of shady characters and the crime syndicate Crimson Dawn in the hope of making his fortune. He uses his gunslinger skills to fight, steal, and scam his way through life.

Double holster carries two guns for ambidextrous Beckett

Tobias and Val look forward to a time when it will just be the two of them together.

RSKF-44 heavy blaster

Muddy Thieves

Beckett and his crew of outlaws are posing as Imperial troopers on Mimban when they meet Han Solo and Chewbacca. Beckett has plans to steal an AT-hauler from a busy airfield for use in an upcoming job.

A SEASONED

scoundrel, Beckett pulls off such ambitious heists that he needs a crew to help him, but he never lets his guard down with them. His motto is: assume everyone will betray you and you'll never be disappointed. This is also good advice for anyone who knows him.

TORO CALICAN

BOUNTY HUNTER IN TRAINING

DATA FILE

AFFILIATION: Bounty hunters
HOMEWORLD: Unknown
SPECIES: Human
HEIGHT: 1.75m
(5ft 9in)
APPEARANCES: M
SEE ALSO: Fennec
Shand; the
Mandalorian; Tusken
Raider

Blaster pistol

NEW BOUNTY HUNTER Toro Calican is determined to prove himself as one of the very best. Young and ambitious, Toro wants to join the Bounty Hunters Guild and partners with the Mandalorian to help achieve this goal.

Neck buff paired with racing goggles offers protection from elements

WHAT TORO lacks in experience he makes up for in reckless enthusiasm. When he meets the Mandalorian on Tatooine, Toro offers him all of his credits in exchange for his help in tracking down Fennec Shand. Her capture could secure his place in the Bounty Hunters Guild.

New leather holster and belt

Toro rents an old speeder bike to seek the assassin Fennec Shand among Tatooine's desert dunes.

A Dangerous Conversation

While secured as Toro Calican's prisoner, Fennec Shand tells him that if he will let her go, she will pay him double and they can team up against Mando— also a valuable prize. He suspects Fennec will try to best him and so blasts her instead of working with her.

Tightly buckled trouser legs prevent trips

TRUDGEN

KNIGHT OF REN TROPHY COLLECTOR

DATA FILE

AFFILIATION: Knights of Ren
HOMEWORLD: Unknown
SPECIES: Unknown
HEIGHT: 1.75m (5ft 9in)
APPEARANCES: VII, IX
SEE ALSO: Ap'lek; Cardo; Kuruk; Kylo Ren; Ushar; Vicrul

Hood taken from a beast master

TRUDGEN HAS MADE IT a personal mission to be the last to leave a fight so he can collect trophies from his victims. He customizes his clothing with these macabre fragments. Trudgen's enormous vibrocleaver fills his opponents with dread.

Vibrocleaver

THE KNIGHTS

of Ren modify ancient weapons to increase their destructiveness. Ultrasonic technology in Trudgen's vibrocleaver allows the blade to rapidly vibrate, which magnifies its lethal cutting power.

Weapons belt

Final Battle

After Ben Solo embraces the light side of the Force, the Knights of Ren return to Exegol and their powerful master, Palpatine. The Knights are a formidable threat to Ben until Rey sends him the Skywalker lightsaber.

Trudgen's helmet includes trophies from a defeated death trooper.

Secondary blade

TUSKEN RAIDER

FIERCE TATOOINIAN NOMADS

DATA FILE

AFFILIATION: None
HOMEWORLD: Tatooine
SPECIES: Tusken
HEIGHT: Varies
APPEARANCES: I, II, IV, M
SEE ALSO: Anakin Skywalker

Gaderffii stick made
from scavenged metal

Eye-
protection
lenses

Anakin Skywalker
releases his vengeful
fury on the Tusken
encampment.

Moisture trap

TUSKEN RAIDERS, OR

Sand People, are seen as
fierce nomads by some who
live on Tatooine. They prowl
remote areas, surviving
where no others can. In rare
instances, the Tuskens are
willing to work with settlers,
even though they see
them as invaders on
their homeworld.

SAND PEOPLE

wear heavy clothing to protect
them from the planet's harsh suns.
They keep their faces hidden
behind head bandages. Their
traditional weapon is an ax,
named a gaderffii (or "gaffi stick").

Thick desert robe

During an attack,
Tuskens often wield
stolen weapons.

Silent Attackers

Sand People are often taller than
humans, yet they blend into the
landscape with unsettling ease.
They sometimes scavenge or steal
from the edges of settlement zones.
Only the sound of the feared krayt
dragon is enough to scare the
Sand People away.

TWO TUBES

TOGNATH EGGMATES AND MERCENARIES

DATA FILE

AFFILIATION: Saw Gerrera's Partisans
HOMEWORLD: Yar Togna
SPECIES: Tognath
HEIGHT: 1.9m (6ft 3in)
APPEARANCES: (Benthic) S, RO; (Edrio) RO
SEE ALSO: Saw Gerrera

Exoskeleton skull

Before joining Saw's group, Benthic spent time as one of Enfys Nest's Cloud-Riders.

Sniper's monocular scope

Cannisters of explosives

TOUGH, RUTHLESS mercenaries, Edrio and Benthic serve in Saw Gerrera's militia. They both get called "Two Tubes" because of the breathing devices they wear in oxygen-rich atmospheres.

PART MAMMAL

and part insect, Tognaths have both endo- and exoskeletons, and they see with insectoid compound eyes. In order to operate on a planet like Jedha, they have cybernetic implants to improve their hearing and balance.

Rifle bought on the black market

Eggmates

Tognath start life growing in eggs suspended in jelly. Sometimes these eggs fuse together, creating a strong connection between Tognath that lasts for life. Eggmates do not necessarily have the same parents, but their bond is stronger than normal siblings and can even be telepathic.

UGNAUGHT

PORCINE SPECIES ON CLOUD CITY

DATA FILE

AFFILIATION: None
HOMEWORLD: Gentes
SPECIES: Ugnaught
HEIGHT (AVG.): 1m
(3ft 3in)
APPEARANCES: V, VI, M
SEE ALSO: Kuiil

LONG AGO, many Ugnaughts were enslaved and taken away from their homeworld. The eccentric explorer Lord Ecclessis Figg forced three enslaved Ugnaught tribes to help build Cloud City on Bespin. He later freed them, and they live in the city.

Tusks used in blood duels

Captain's stripes

AN UGNAUGHT named Yoxgit began a life away from Cloud City. He made a fortune illegally selling tibanna gas to arms dealers, then jumped the planet for Tatooine, where he found work with Jabba the Hutt.

Flight gauntlets

Cloud City Workers

Ugnaught workers in the depths of Cloud City sort through discarded metal junk, where C-3PO nearly ends up after he is blasted to pieces. The species has constructed a network of humid, red-lighted work corridors and tunnels throughout the city, most of which can only be navigated by Ugnaughts.

Expensive tactical boots

Ugnaughts perform the often dangerous work of mining and processing tibanna gas.

UNKAR PLUTT

JUNK BOSS OF JAKKU

DATA FILE

AFFILIATION: None
HOMEWORLD: Jakku
SPECIES: Crolute
HEIGHT: 1.8m (5ft 11in)
APPEARANCES: VII
SEE ALSO: BB-8; Rey;
Teedo

UNKAR RUNS a profitable business stealing, scavenging, and selling scrap on Jakku. He doles out slim servings of food in exchange for valuable salvage and calls upon leg-breakers and thugs to ensure he gets the best deals.

Buoyant, gelatinous body tissue

Apron made from salvaged hull plates

UNKAR OPERATES

out of a converted cargo crawler in a large structure at Niima Outpost. He has a monopoly on food vending in the town, and scavengers are forced to barter with him, exchanging valuable salvage for dehydrated food rations.

Boots conceal flipper-like limbs

Fish Out of Water

Unkar is an aquatic Crolute, but his greed keeps him far from the oceans of his homeworld and on Jakku, where he reigns as the undisputed junk boss. The scavenger named Rey is one of his favorite traders. When she disappoints him by backing out of a deal, Unkar takes it badly, and sends his goons to teach her a lesson.

USHAR

SAVAGE KNIGHT OF REN

Airtight helmet

THE CRUELEST Knight of Ren, Ushar savors close combat and makes every battle personal. He judges the fighting spirit of his adversaries and offers a quick death only to those brave enough to fight back.

Thermal detonator

War club

USHAR CARRIES a range of weapons, including a war club for close combat. This fearsome weapon is enhanced at one end with a concussion-field generator. Powered by kinetite, a form of lightning generated by the Force, it can produce widely dispersed, destructive shockwaves.

To Serve

To join the ranks of the Knights of Ren, candidates must have a connection to "the shadow," or the dark side of the Force. They must also be willing to kill at great personal sacrifice. Those found unworthy of joining the Knights do not survive for long.

Battle stance

Ushar's helmet filters out air, a sign that he is an alien.

Filthy footwear

VAL

WEAPONS EXPERT

DATA FILE

AFFILIATION: Tobias Beckett's crew; Crimson Dawn
HOMEWORLD: Unknown
SPECIES: Human
HEIGHT: 1.57m (5ft 2in)
APPEARANCES: S
SEE ALSO: Rio Durant; Tobias Beckett

Cables carry a current that jams signal detectors

During a failed attempt to secure coaxium, Val sacrifices herself in the explosion on Vandor.

A LONGTIME member of Tobias Beckett's criminal crew, Val has survived many risky ventures. She is a tough, no-nonsense weapons expert and an ace shot with a blaster rifle.

Climbing gloves have an electro-magnetic grip

VAL IS VERY

secretive about her past. Practically all anyone knows is that her father was a musician who named her after the Valachord instrument. Val is in love with Tobias Beckett, but she does not even share her secrets with him.

Syntherope for climbing

Crack Bomb Maker

Val uses her knowledge of chemistry and electronics to create explosives. For the coaxium heist on Vandor, she makes a baradium bomb to blow up the conveyex transport. The detonator is keyed to her biological signature so only she can set it off.

VALIN HESS

CRUEL IMPERIAL GENERAL

DATA FILE

AFFILIATION: Empire; Imperial Remnant
HOMEWORLD: Unknown
SPECIES: Human
HEIGHT: 1.88m (6ft 2in)
APPEARANCES: M
SEE ALSO: The Mandalorian; Migs Mayfeld; Stormtrooper

Command disk

ONCE A GREAT Imperial general, Valin Hess refuses to give up on his ideals. Hess still believes in the Empire's mission to bring order to the galaxy, no matter who is hurt or put in danger—even if that is Hess' own soldiers.

Imperial rank plaque

Communications belt

At-ease position

VALIN HESS is unrepentantly responsible for destroying an entire city because it resisted the Empire. He holds no regrets, even though 5,000–10,000 of his own troops were there. To Hess, soldiers are expendable.

Hess sits in the mess hall on the Morak base, registering that the heroic pilots have just entered.

An Uncomfortable Conversation

Valin Hess brags about the destruction he caused during Operation: Cinder, which killed sharpshooter Migs Mayfeld's fellow soldiers and friends. He does not realize that Mayfeld is still angry about what happened until it is too late.

Imperial-issue boots

VICE ADMIRAL HOLDO

NOBLE RESISTANCE COMMANDER

DATA FILE

AFFILIATION: Resistance
HOMEWORLD: Gatalenta
SPECIES: Human
HEIGHT: 1.78m (5ft 10in)
APPEARANCES: VIII
SEE ALSO: Poe Dameron;
Princess Leia

Dyed hair is part of
her unique style

VICE ADMIRAL Amilyn Holdo is a longtime friend and comrade of Leia Organa's. When Leia is injured, Holdo takes command of her MC85 Star Cruiser, the *Raddus*. It is one of only three remaining Resistance ships.

Gatalentan-style
draped gown

Gatalentan bracelets

Defender-5
sporting blaster

HOLDO carries with her the independent and offbeat spirit of her home planet, Gatalenta. She wears her own style of clothes rather than following military uniform. Meditation and astrology bring a calmness to her military strategy. Her ultimate sacrifice enables the few remaining fighters to escape. Thanks to her, the spark of hope lives on.

Unassuming Hero

Holdo is an astute, levelheaded commander, but her secretive manner leads to some tension. Poe Dameron even attempts a mutiny. Modest and dedicated, Holdo is more interested in protecting the Resistance than appearing a hero. And when she sacrifices herself, Poe sees her for the hero that she is.

Holdo goes down with her ship, but takes out the *Supremacy* with it.

VICRUL

Helmet
strikes fear
in prey

Curved vibroblade

DATA FILE

AFFILIATION: Knights of Ren
HOMEWORLD:
Unknown
SPECIES: Unknown
HEIGHT: 1.79m (5ft 10in)
APPEARANCES: VII, IX
SEE ALSO: Ap'lek;
Cardo; Kuruk; Kylo Ren;
Trudgen; Ushar

VICRUL SEEKS out conflict in the belief that he gains power from every victim he defeats. He experiences surges of uncontrollable dark-side Force energy in combat, which make him an even more monstrous fighter.

Spiked wrist guard for
wounding opponents

THE FORCE abilities of all the Knights of Ren are limited as they have not received proper training to control their powers. Vicrul's Force sensitivity heightens his reflexes and enables him to magnify fear in his prey.

Combat pants

Vicrul's vibroscythe has a vibrating edge for extra cutting power.

Cruel Marauders

For centuries, dark tales of the Knights of Ren spread throughout the Unknown Regions. The Knights thrive on inciting chaos and live by a code where they do what they please without mercy.

271

VOBER DAND

RESISTANCE GROUND CONTROLLER

DATA FILE

AFFILIATION: Resistance
HOMEWORLD: Suntilla
SPECIES: Tarsunt
HEIGHT: 1.73m (5ft 8in)
APPEARANCES: VII, VIII, IX
SEE ALSO: Nien Nunb;
PZ-4CO

Comlink headset

GLD controller's coat

STAYING EVER mobile and out of reach of First Order reprisals, the Resistance uses forgotten bases that were originally built as rebel outposts during the Galactic Civil War. These old, austere facilities ask much from the Resistance's hard-pressed ground personnel.

DURING THE Starkiller crisis, Vober Dand manages the ground crews that maintain the fleet of X-wings at the D'Qar outpost. The hard-nosed Tarsunt runs a tight operation, demanding the best of his teams of mechanics and support staff. Though it's the pilots who get the glory, Dand knows they would be grounded if not for his efforts.

Without the deep finances and government supplies of the New Republic, Vober Dand must keep the Resistance's small fleet of X-wings flying at all hours.

Logistics Chief

In the loose-knit Resistance organization, Vober Dand holds the rank of chief of Ground Logistics Division. He is one of the first Resistance members consulted when establishing a new base, using his mathematical mind to calculate the specifics of flight schedules, maintenance requirements, and hangar operations.

WAT TAMBOR

EMIR AND FOREMAN OF THE TECHNO UNION

DATA FILE

AFFILIATION: Techno Union; Separatists
HOMEWORLD: Skako
SPECIES: Skakoan
HEIGHT: 1.93m (6ft 4in)
APPEARANCES: II, III
SEE ALSO: Boba Fett; Darth Vader

Darth Vader shows no mercy to Wat Tambor on Mustafar.

Vocabulator/
annunciator

Rich outer tunic
over pressure suit

Dials control
vocabulator

WAT TAMBOR IS FOREMAN
of the Techno Union, a
powerful commercial body
that makes massive profits
from new technologies.
He is also an executive
of arms manufacturer,
Baktoid Armor Workshop.

TAMBOR LEFT his home
planet Skako at an early age and
began a career in technology
on the harsh industrial world of
Metalorn. Few Skakoans leave
their world, due to its unique
atmospheric pressure. In fact,
Tambor must wear a special
suit to avoid his body
exploding in standard,
oxygen-based atmospheres.

Raiding Ryloth

During the Clone Wars, Tambor oversees
the sacking of Ryloth, homeworld of the
Twi'leks. Tambor and his droid army
hold the capital city, Lessu, until they
are pushed out during a counterattack
by General Mace Windu. Tambor is
then captured and imprisoned.

WATTO

TOYDARIAN JUNK DEALER

DATA FILE

AFFILIATION: None
HOMEWORLD: Toydaria
SPECIES: Toydarian
HEIGHT: 1.37m (4ft 6in)
APPEARANCES: I, II
SEE ALSO: Anakin Skywalker;
Qui-Gon Jinn; Shmi
Skywalker

WATTO IS A QUICK-WITTED, flying Toydarian shopkeeper who owns a spare parts business in Mos Eisley on Tatooine. He spends his proceeds at podraces, gambling with Hutts, and purchasing enslaved individuals—including Anakin and Shmi Skywalker.

Flexible, trunk-like nose

Watto insists his shop is a parts dealership, though most would call it a junk shop.

Three-day stubble

WATTO was a soldier on his homeworld Toydaria, but left the planet after suffering an injury. On Tatooine, he watched how the Jawas sold used goods, learning some of their tricks before setting up his own business.

Large belly mostly composed of gas

Keycodes for main safe and slave keepers

Watto is surprised that Anakin Skywalker is now a Jedi.

Chance Meeting

When Watto meets an offworlder looking for spare hyperdrive parts, he sees an opportunity for some profitable swindling. Jedi Qui-Gon Jinn does not suspect that he will meet the prophesied Chosen One, Anakin Skywalker, in this very shop. After Anakin is freed, Watto's business suffers, and it is the start of a downward spiral for the enslaver.

WEDGE ANTILLES

REBELLION HERO

X-WING PILOT Wedge Antilles has flown on missions for the Rebel Alliance, the New Republic and the Resistance. His ability to keep a cool head, even in the most lopsided battles, makes him a legend among other pilots.

X-wing pilot flight suit

MORE AT HOME in the air than on the ground, Wedge trains at an Imperial academy before defecting to the Rebel Alliance. He and Luke Skywalker are the only X-wing pilots who survive the assault on the first Death Star. Wedge goes on to fly in the battles of Hoth, Endor, and Jakku.

One of 12 flight helmets Wedge owns

Wedge joins the Resistance's fight against the First Order.

Born to Fly

After helping destroy two Death Stars, Wedge assists in the training of a new generation of pilots, including Temmin "Snap" Wexley. Wedge goes on to marry Temmin's mother, and fellow pilot, Norra. The couple retires from flying until the Resistance calls for their help. Wedge flies once more at the Battle of Exegol.

Signal flares

Boots worn at Battle of Endor

WICKET W. WARRICK

YOUNG EWOK LONER

DATA FILE

AFFILIATION: Bright Tree Village

HOMEWORLD: Forest Moon of Endor

SPECIES: Ewok

HEIGHT: 80cm (2ft 7in)

APPEARANCES: VI, IX

SEE ALSO: Chief Chirpa; Logray; Princess Leia; Teebo

Spear

Hood

Thick fur

An older Wicket and his son Pommet watch gleefully as a Star Destroyer is annihilated.

WICKET W. WARRICK

is a young Ewok with a reputation as a loner. He spends much time wandering far from his village in the forests of Endor's moon. Wicket is on one of his travels when he runs into Princess Leia Organa. He helps her to the safety of his treetop village, and soon comes to trust her.

Friends?

Wicket bonds with Leia, and when her friends arrive, he argues that they should be spared any abuse. But his solitary habits leave him with a big lack of influence among the elders in Bright Tree Village.

YOUNG Wicket had an adventurous childhood with his great friends—Teebo, Kneesaa, Paploo, and his brothers Weechee and Willy. Though Wicket respects the mystic shamanic magic employed by Logray, he does not possess the patience to practice it.

WINTA

LOYAL FRIEND

DATA FILE

AFFILIATION: Unknown
HOMEWORLD: Sorgan
SPECIES: Human
HEIGHT: Unknown
APPEARANCES: M
SEE ALSO: Grogu; the
Mandalorian; Omera

The children in Winta's village are happy to make a new friend when Grogu comes to town.

Weatherproof tunic

WINTA LIVES in a small village on the planet Sorgan with her mother, Omera. She becomes good friends with Grogu when he arrives. Winta feels protective of the Child and will do everything she can to keep him safe.

Belt made
by her mother

WINTA AND her mother are farming for krill one day when they are surprised by a group of vicious Klatooinian raiders attacking their village. They stay safe by hiding under a fishing basket in a pond until the raiders are gone.

A Sad Goodbye

Grogu and the Mandalorian have to leave Sorgan because the Child is being pursued by bounty hunters. Winta and Grogu have a great bond, and Winta is sad to see her new friend leave, even though she knows it is for the best.

Farming work boots

DATA FILE

AFFILIATION: Rebel Alliance; New Republic; Resistance
HOMEWORLD: Various
SPECIES: Various
HEIGHT: Varies
STANDARD VEHICLE: X-wing starfighter
APPEARANCES: RO, IV, V, VI, M, VII, VIII, IX
SEE ALSO: Luke Skywalker; Poe Dameron

HEROIC X-WING pilots are the stuff of legend. Rebel Alliance pilots fly X-wing starfighters against the Empire. New Republic X-wing patrols try to maintain law in the galaxy. Later, when the Resistance is battling the First Order, its pilots draw on the same uniforms and traditions.

IN THE EARLY days of the Rebel Alliance, X-wing pilots like Major Ralo Surrel are based on the Massassi outpost on Yavin 4. They fly T-65 X-wings in the first incarnations of the soon-to-be legendary Red, Blue, Green, and Gold Squadrons.

Life-support unit

Equipment pocket

Gear harness

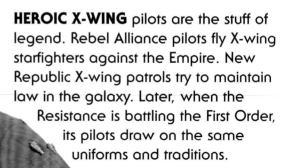

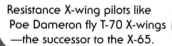

Resistance X-wing pilots like Poe Dameron fly T-70 X-wings —the successor to the X-65.

Battle of Yavin

Pilots of Red Squadron such as Wedge Antilles ("Red Two"), Biggs Darklighter ("Red Three"), and Luke Skywalker ("Red Five") are crucial to the destruction of the first Death Star. Antilles and Skywalker are the only two who survive.

XI'AN

WARRIOR TWI'LEK

Headgear contains communicator

XI'AN AND her twin brother Qin are part of Ranzar Malk's mercenary crew. She has an explosive personality and a hot temper and is more likely to resolve a disagreement with her throwing knives than with words.

False Smiles

Xi'an enjoys reminding Din Djarin of a time in their past when they worked together. Yet Xi'an blames the Mandalorian for her brother's imprisonment by the New Republic and waits patiently for her chance at revenge.

Arm sleeve hides weapons

Silent throwing knife

Flexible clothing allows for optimum agility in combat

Compartments hold extra throwing knives

WHILE SOME Twi'leks, such as Jedi Aayla Secura and rebel Hera Syndulla, risked their lives to fight against tyranny, others like Xi'an turned to a life of crime in the murky underworld.

Xi'an embraces her brother, Qin, as they are reunited aboard a New Republic prison ship.

YADDLE

COMPASSIONATE JEDI MASTER

SITTING ON THE Jedi High Council, Master Yaddle offers few words but much compassion and balanced patience. She looks up to Master Yoda, who is of the same species as her but is almost twice her age (Yaddle is a mere 477 years old).

Mind and Body

Yaddle has devoted a lot of time to scholarly interests, and spends much time in the Jedi Archives. But she has been an active Jedi in the field, too.

YADDLE has trained many Jedi Padawans, including fellow Council member Oppo Rancisis.

Youthful topknot

Shapely ears

YARAEL POOF

QUERMIAN JEDI MASTER

DATA FILE

AFFILIATION: Jedi
HOMEWORLD: Quermia
SPECIES: Quermian
HEIGHT: 2.64m (8ft 8in)
APPEARANCES: 1
SEE ALSO: Obi-Wan Kenobi;
Qui-Gon Jinn

Extended
neck

Traditional
Quermian
cannom collar

JEDI MASTER Yarael Poof
has been a member of
the High Council for
centuries by the time
of the Naboo Crisis.
He is a master of
specialized Jedi
mind tricks,
which he can
use to bring
conflicts to a
decisive end.

Deceptive Appearances

Yarael Poof quietly watches the
proceedings as Qui-Gon Jinn
and Obi-Wan Kenobi report from
their mission to Naboo. Though
appearing as a serene thinker
among the Jedi Council
members, Master Yarael is a
dexterous combatant with a
lightsaber, and has perfected
many incredible moves
that only his spineless
anatomy can allow.

Poof has a
mischievous
side and enjoys
playing mind tricks
on colleagues.

QUERMIANS HAVE

extended necks and long limbs,
as well as a second pair of arms,
which Poof hides under his Jedi
robe. The species is noseless, as
Quermians smell with olfactory
glands in their hands. They also have
two brains—an upper brain in the
head and a lower brain in the chest.

Robe hides
second pair of
arms and chest
with lower brain

YODA

LEGENDARY JEDI MASTER

DATA FILE

AFFILIATION: Jedi
HOMEWORLD: Unknown
SPECIES: Unknown
HEIGHT: 66cm (2ft 2in)
APPEARANCES: I, II, III, V, VI, VIII
SEE ALSO: Luke Skywalker

Head has been nearly bald for centuries

Homespun robe

YODA IS ONE OF THE most powerful Jedi ever, and has lived to be 900 years old. He served the Galactic Republic at its height, as well as through its decline and fall. Yoda is one of the few Jedi to survive the Clone Wars. He goes into hiding on the remote planet Dagobah.

Sith Fury

Finally accepting that the Clone Wars have been nothing more than a manipulation by the Sith to destroy the Jedi Order, Yoda confronts Palpatine. Even the Jedi's amazing strength and speed, however, are not a match for the devastating fury of a Sith Lord.

YODA HAS

guided hundreds of Jedi to knighthood and visited countless worlds. He takes quiet satisfaction in his ability to resolve conflict by nonviolent means, until the re-emergence of the dark side unseats others' confidence in him.

On Dagobah, Yoda trains Luke Skywalker, his final student and the galaxy's last hope.

Anakin, Yoda, and Obi-Wan Kenobi become one with the Force after their deaths.

ZAM WESELL

SHAPE-CHANGING ASSASSIN

KYD-21
blaster

ZAM WESELL is a hired assassin with a special edge. As a Clawdite shape-shifter, Wesell can change her appearance to mimic that of other species. For some years, Zam has worked with renowned bounty hunter Jango Fett.

Bodysuit stretches to
allow shape-shifting

Direct-to-lungs
breathpack

Blast-energy skirt

ZAM WESELL

was born on Zolan, the home of the Mabari, an ancient order of warrior-knights. The Mabari trained Zam until her desire for wealth took her to the vast metropolis of Denon, where she employed her skills and training as an assassin.

Airspeeder Chase

Zam Wesell often steals a new vehicle for each job, to avoid being traced. But she uses her own airspeeder when she knows she needs to get away fast. When Zam takes on a job for Jango Fett—to kill Senator Padmé Amidala—she has to outrun two Jedi Knights in a borrowed speeder who are hard on her trail.

Boots accept
a variety of
limb forms

In her true Clawdite form, Zam Wesell is a reptilian humanoid.

ZORII BLISS

RESILIENT SPICE RUNNER

DATA FILE

AFFILIATION: Spice Runners of Kijimi
HOMEWORLD: Kijimi
SPECIES: Human
HEIGHT: 1.62m (5ft 4in)
APPEARANCES: IX
SEE ALSO: Babu Frik; Poe Dameron; Rey

Helmet includes life-support system

Bronzium gorget

Arm guard deflects blaster fire

ZORII JOINED THE

Spice Runners as a teenager, when her mother, Zeva Bliss, led the criminal gang. After Poe Dameron and Zorii foil Zeva's plan to assassinate her rivals, Poe leaves the Spice Runners while Zorii eventually becomes the gang's leader.

Zorii carries twin E-851 blasters

Custom spacer's boots

Zorii shares her plan to escape Kijimi with Poe and asks if he wants to join her.

ZORII BLISS IS the fierce leader of the Spice Runners of Kijimi, a local criminal gang. She reluctantly agrees to help Poe Dameron, who abruptly left the Spice Runners to join the Resistance, when he returns to Kijimi.

Mutual Respect

Zorii is initially angered by Poe's return to Kijimi, but she admires Rey's fighting skills and her direct plea for help. Zorii later gives Poe a First Order officer's transit data-medallion so he and Rey can attempt to rescue Chewbacca from the orbiting Star Destroyer.

ZUCKUSS

GAND BOUNTY HUNTER

DATA FILE

AFFILIATION: Bounty hunter
HOMEWORLD: Gand
SPECIES: Gand
HEIGHT: 1.5m (4ft 11in)
APPEARANCES: V
SEE ALSO: 4-LOM

Compound eyes

Ammonia respirator

Heavy battle armor under robe

Breather packs

ZUCKUSS IS an insectoid Gand bounty hunter who often partners with droid bounty hunter 4-LOM. Zuckuss is a tireless tracker, who uses the mystic findsman traditions that date back centuries on his fog-shrouded homeworld, Gand.

ZUCKUSS breathes only ammonia, so he wears a respirator in oxygen-based atmospheres. When his planet's findsman traditions began dying out, Zuckuss became one of the first findsmen to go offworld. Bounty hunting is now a lucrative way for him to use his particular talents.

Zuckuss is renowned for his tracking skills and is a highly sought-after bounty hunter.

Findsman body cloak

Powerful Pair

Zuckuss' uncanny abilities make other bounty hunters uneasy. But not 4-LOM, whom Zuckuss partners with many times. The two bounty hunters make a formidable team. The pairing does not go unnoticed by Darth Vader, who hires them to locate the *Millennium Falcon*.

INDEX

ACKNOWLEDGMENTS

 Penguin Random House

Project Editor Matt Jones
Project Art Editor Chris Gould
Production Editor Marc Staples
Senior Producer Mary Slater
Managing Editors Emma Grange and Sarah Harland
Managing Art Editor Vicky Short
Publishing Director Mark Searle

Edited for DK by Simon Beecroft and Shari Last
Designed for DK by Gareth Butterworth

For Lucasfilm
Senior Editor Brett Rector
Creative Director of Publishing Michael Siglain
Art Director Troy Alders
Art Department Phil Szostak
Story Group Pablo Hidalgo, Leland Chee, Emily Shkoukani
Asset Management Chris Argyropoulos, Jackey Cabrera,
Gabrielle Levenson, Bryce Pinkos, Erik Sanchez,
Jason Schultz, Sarah Williams

DK would like to thank Chelsea Alon at Disney Publishing; Vicky Armstrong
and Cefn Ridout for editorial assistance; Vanessa Bird for the index;
Megan Douglass for proofreading and Americanization; Julia March and
Louise Stevenson for proofreading and Anglicization; Neha Ahuja,
Owen Bennett, Dan Bunyan, Jo Casey, Elizabeth Dowsett, David Fentiman,
Julie Ferris, Jon Hall, Guy Harvey, Akansha Jain, Tori Kosara, Lisa Lanzarini,
David McDonald, Clare Millar, Lynne Moulding, Lauren Nesworthy,
Mark Penfound, Sandra Perry, Clive Savage, Sadie Smith, Lisa Sodeau,
Ron Stobbart, Chitra Subramanyam, Rhys Thomas, Toby Truphet,
and Arushi Vats for their work on previous editions of this book.

This American Edition, 2021
First American Edition, 2011
Published in the United States by DK Publishing
1745 Broadway, 20th Floor, New York NY 10019

© & TM 2021 LUCASFILM LTD.

Page Design Copyright © 2011, 2021 Dorling Kindersley Limited
DK, a Division of Penguin Random House LLC
23 24 25 10 9 8 7 6 5
013–326318–Nov/2021

A catalog record for this book
is available from the Library of Congress.
ISBN 978-0-7440-5031-8

DK books are available at special discounts when purchased
in bulk for sales promotions, premiums, fund-raising, or educational use.
For details, contact: DK Publishing Special Markets,
1745 Broadway, 20th Floor, New York NY 10019
SpecialSales@dk.com

Printed and bound in China

For the curious

www.dk.com
www.starwars.com

 MIX
Paper from
responsible sources
FSC™ C018179

This book is made from
Forest Stewardship Council™
certified paper—one small
step in DK's commitment
to a sustainable future.